THE GOSPEL ACCORDING TO MARK:

A WALK IN THE WORD

by

Dana Kruckenberg Thompson

Gotham Books

30 N Gould St.
Ste. 20820, Sheridan, WY 82801
https://gothambooksinc.com/

Phone: 1 (307) 464-7800

© 2024 *Dana Kruckenberg Thompson.* All rights reserved.

No part of this book may be reproduced, stored in a retrieval system, or transmitted by any means without the written permission of the author.

Published by Gotham Books (September 6, 2024)

ISBN: 979-8-3304-0151-2 (P)
ISBN: 979-8-3304-0152-9 (E)

Because of the dynamic nature of the Internet, any web addresses or links contained in this book may have changed since publication and may no longer be valid.

The views expressed in this work are solely those of the author and do not necessarily reflect the views of the publisher, and the publisher hereby disclaims any responsibility for them.

Contents

Introduction iv

Lesson One: Mark 1:1-20 1

Lesson Two: Mark 1:21-45 7

Lesson Three: Mark 2 14

Lesson Four: Mark 3 22

Lesson Five: Mark 4 29

Lesson Six: Mark 5:1-20 36

Lesson Seven: Mark 5:21-43 45

Lesson Eight: Mark 6:1-29 52

Lesson Nine: Mark 6:30-56 58

Lesson Ten: Mark 7 66

Lesson Eleven: Mark 8 73

Lesson Twelve: Mark 9:1-29 80

Lesson Thirteen: Mark 9:30-50 85

Lesson Fourteen: Mark 10:1-27 94

Lesson Fifteen: Mark 10:28-52 101

Lesson Sixteen: Mark 11 110

Lesson Seventeen: Mark 12 118

Lesson Eighteen: Mark 13 128

Lesson Nineteen: Mark 14:1-26 137

Lesson Twenty: Mark 14:27-52 145

Lesson Twenty-One: Mark 15:1-24 153

Lesson Twenty-Two: Mark 15:25-47 161

Lesson Twenty-Three: Mark 16 170

A Walk in The Word

The Gospel According to Mark
A Study by Dana Kruckenberg Thompson

Introduction

> "The Son of Man came not to be ministered unto, but to minister, and to give his life as a ransom for many."
>
> – Mark 10:45

This verse is the key to the presentation of our Lord Jesus Christ in Mark's gospel.

In the chapters of this fast-paced book, Jesus is not presented as Prophet, Priest, or King, but as a servant, the Servant of Jehovah. In order for Jesus to fulfill these other exalted roles, it behooved Him to humble Himself, to take on the form of a servant, to act in absolute obedience, even unto death, the death of the cross.

There is no genealogy given for Jesus in this gospel, for the simple reason that a servant's blood lineage is of no consequence. What concerns a person who employs a servant are his references and record of service. Is the servant able to perform his duties satisfactorily? In Marks' gospel, which shows our Savior moving from one might deed to the next, we see that He is more than able; indeed, as Ephesians 3:20 states, Jesus is "able to do exceeding abundantly above all that we ask or think." God the Father made his approbation clear from the beginning of Jesus' ministry. At His baptism, it was the Father who said from heaven, "Thou art my beloved Son, in whom I am well pleased."

Not only was Jesus qualified to serve as He walked the earth, but He is qualified to save as no other individual has been, or ever will be. Only the Perfect One, the sinless God-Man, could bridge the gap of sin for us. He came down from the indescribable glory of Heaven, where He was continually worshipped, to become man, to be rejected and despised for you, and for me. How can we not love Him with all our being? How can we neglect to praise His Name daily?

To develop a Christ-like character is the goal of every sincere believer. We desire the love, serenity, wisdom, gentleness, and righteousness of Jesus. But how deeply do we desire the life of service presented in this gospel? Are we willing to serve all men in Jesus' Name and for His glory? Ours is a society full of lepers, riddled with physical and moral disease resulting from sin. Will you touch these lepers with the gospel of Christ that they might become clean? A life of ministry is available to you – will you rise "a great deal before day"[1] to seek it?

As we engulf ourselves in the life and ministry of Jesus, let us fall in love with Him again and absorb His character into our own! Give your whole life to Jesus to do with as He wills. Make a commitment today to discover your ministry and to use it to the edifying of the church and the saving of souls. For even the Son of Man came not to be ministered unto, but to minister, and to give his life as a ransom for many.

---

[1] Mark 1:35.

Lesson One: Mark 1:1-20

Read Mark 1:1-20

Please **pray** before answering the questions.

1. What is "the Gospel"? Answer in your own words.

   Look up and write these Scriptures:

   1Timothy 1:15:

   Acts 2:21

   Romans 10:9

2. At what point did the Gospel of Jesus Christ begin?
   (See Micah 5:2 & Revelation 13:8)

   Discuss these scriptures also:

   Genesis 3:14-15:

   2 Samuel 7:12-13&16:

   Revelation 22:16

   Job 19:25

   Psalm 69:7-9

Dana Kruckenberg Thompson

    Psalm 68:2-3

    Isaiah 53:5-6&12:

3. Which prophecies were made concerning John the Baptist?

    Malachi 3:1:

    Isaiah 40:3:

    Luke 1:13-17:

    Why is this so crucial?

    Summarize 1 Corinthians 15:13-23 in your own words.

4. Describe John and his ministry. (v. 4-6; see also Luke 3:7-14)
5. What was John's attitude toward Christ? (v. 7-8)

Ask yourself in the presence of God, "Am I willing to give the Lord Jesus the pre-eminence in everything, to let Him be glorified, and myself perhaps not even noticed?"

6. When was the prophecy in verse 8 fulfilled?

    How was the prophecy originally worded in the Old Testament?

        Isaiah 44:3:

Joel 2:28-29:

7. Describe the baptism of Jesus (v. 9-11).

   Did Jesus need to be baptized?
   (See Matthew 3:14-15; 2 Corinthians 5:21; Hebrews 7:25-26)

8. How did God the Father show His pleasure at the humility and obedience of His Son?
   (v. 10-11)

   How do the following verses say we can please God?

   Proverbs 3:1-4:

   Hebrews 11:6:

   Colossians 1:10:

   1 John 3:22:

9. Look up these texts that prove the existence of the Trinity:

   Acts 2:33:

   2 Corinthians 13:14:

   1 Timothy 3:16:

   Hebrews 9:14:

1 John 5:6-7:

10. What happened to Jesus immediately after His baptism?

   Can we expect to be attacked by Satan after a Spiritual Victory? Why? (See 1 Peter 5:8)

   Discuss Satan's variety of temptations from reading Luke 4:2-13.

11. Which temptations are you most susceptible to?

   Using Jesus' example, how should a Christian reply to Satan's enticing half-truths and misquoted scriptures? (See also Ephesians 6:10-11 & 17; Hebrews 4:12)

12. What happened to John the Baptist? (See Matthew 14:3-12)

   When John's ministry was concluded, what had he said of himself in relationship to Jesus? (See John 3:30)

13. What was Jesus' message? (v. 14-15)

   Describe what the kingdom of God is, using these scriptures:

   Psalm 103:19:

   Luke 17:20b-21:

   Luke 22:29:

Hebrews 1:8:

2 Peter 1:10-11:

Revelation 12:10:

14. Give the meaning of the phrase, "The time is fulfilled" using the following Scriptures:

    Isaiah 61:1-2:

    Luke 4:18-21:

    Daniel 9:24:

    Galatians 4:4-5:

15. How must we respond to the gospel of the kingdom of God?

    2 Corinthians 7:10:

    John 3:3-5:

16. What opportunity did Jesus offer to Simon and Andrew, James & John? (v. 17-19)

    How did they respond?

17. What opportunity does Jesus present to His followers today?

    Mark 16:15:

    Acts 26:18:

    1 Corinthians 16:9:

    Revelation 3:8a:

18. Share the particular way in which God has shown *you* to bring people to Christ.

    How will you respond?

Dear Lord Jesus, as I look at Your life and character, I so desire to be like You, to follow You, to be a servant! Mold me this day, I pray, in Your precious Name.

Lesson Two: Mark 1:21-45

> "And at evening, when the sun did set, they brought unto Him all that were diseased, and them that were possessed with devils… and He healed many that were sick of diverse diseases and cast out many devils."
> - Mark 1:32,34

> "The works which the Father hath given me to finish, the same works that I do, bear witness of me, that the Father hath sent me."
> - John 5:36

> "And in the morning, rising up at great while before day, He went out, and departed into a solitary place, and there prayed."
> - Mark 1:35

As we follow Jesus during this busy day of ministry, we can see the outstanding characteristic of His public demeanor: authority. Jesus had authority in the Word of God, teaching truth, rather than quoting and comparing opinions, as was the habit of the rabbis. He had authority over sickness and disease, healing all who came to Him. He had authority over unclean spirits, those demons who indwell humans in order to torment and destroy them. Mark gives five separate references to the casting out of demons in this half of the chapter alone. Demon possession and oppression are very real afflictions from the devil himself, even in this day of sophistication when labeled "mental illness" and masked with drug injections. The pridefulness of humanistic man will not allow the Name of Jesus to be called upon – Jesus, the One who has complete and ultimate authority over the devil, and who will not fail to answer a prayer of faith.

What was the source of His authority? Jesus Himself made it clear in John 6:38, "For I came down from heaven not to do mine own will, but the will of Him who sent me." Throughout His ministry Jesus continually said that His words and works were not His own, but those of the Father who had sent Him. Jesus' identification and oneness with the Father were so complete that He said, "He that believeth on me, believeth not on me, but on Him that sent me. And he that seeth me seeth Him that sent me… Whatsoever I speak, therefore, even as the Father said unto me, so I speak."[2]

---
[2] John 12:44, 45, 50

How can we proclaim our Heavenly Father as our source of authority as we speak the words of eternal life? How can we do the work of God in such a way as to be able to say, "I do always those things that please Him?" Hence we come to the secret of Jesus' authority, found in verse 35 of our chapter: "And in the morning, rising up a great while before day, He went out, and departed into a solitary place, and there prayed." Jesus Christ, God the Son, in perfect oneness with the Father, yet took time – made time – to communicate with the Father. He worshipped and fellowshipped with the Father, rising in the dark while others slept after a busy day of ministry, with another hectic day ahead. But Jesus knew the secret of true preparation for doing God's work – making time in the presence of God the top priority. When our first activity of the day is prayer to God, all other activities will fall into their rightful place and order. With God-given confidence and Spirit-led authority, we can face challenges to our faith and Christian values, with results that our well-pleasing to God. The Lord may even see fit to use us in a miraculous work of His choosing, for Jesus said, "He that believeth on me, the works that I do shall he do also; and greater works shall he do..."[3]

We can, and should, do great works for God, always going about doing good, speaking the word of truth, destroying the work of the devil wherever we encounter it. But not one thing will we accomplish without applying our Lord's source of power to our lives: prayer to the Father.

Read Mark 1:21-45

Please **pray** for the guidance of the Holy Spirit before you answer the questions.

1. We see the immediacy in v. 21. What did Jesus begin doing in the town of Capernaum?

    What was different about Jesus' teaching? (v.22)
    See also:
    Luke 4:32:

---

[3] John 14:12

Matthew 15:9:

John 7:15-16:

2. Who did Jesus encounter in the Synagogue? (v.23)

Who are the unclean spirits?

See also:
Matthew 12:24:

Jude 6:

Ephesians 6:12:

What did Jesus tell us about unclean spirits?

Matthew 12:28:

Matthew 12:43-45:

Matthew 25:41:

What did the evil spirit know that had not yet been revealed even to the disciples? (v.24; See also Luke 1:35 and James 2:19b)

3. Why did Jesus' fame spread throughout Galilee? (v. 27-28)

*We have seen so many of Jesus' miracles in our Christian lives!
Are you sharing His mighty works with others as a testimony for Christ?
Resolve today to do so with renewed zeal! (Acts 22:15)*

4. Recount the story of Simon's mother-in-law found in v. 30-31.

*Do you need a healing touch today? Ask the Lord Jesus to cast out any unbelief in your heart and ask him for your healing! (See Hebrews 4:16)
Make sure to share what the Lord did for you!*

5. In the evening who came to see Jesus? (v. 32-33)

   Why didn't Jesus allow the demons to speak?

   Luke 4:41:

   John 7:6a:

6. Read v. 35-36 carefully. Where did Jesus place His priority for the day?

   What could He have been doing instead?

   What does this tell us about ordering our day?
7. Look up and write these scriptures about prayer:

   Psalm 5:1-3:

   Psalm 27:8:

   Psalm 63:1:

Psalm 143:8:

Isaiah 55:6:

Lamentations 3:40-41:

Matthew 6:9:

Luke 18:1:

Philippians 4:6:

1 Thessalonians 5:17:

Will you make a commitment today to an early morning quiet time?

8. In verse 38, Jesus speaks of His mission. What is it?

    Isaiah 61:1-2:

    John 1:14,18:

    John 17:1-4:

9. How did the leper in v. 40 show his faith in Jesus? What is faith? Use these scriptures to define:

    1 Thessalonians 2:13:

1 Timothy 4:10:

Hebrews 11:1,6:

Because of your trials, burdens, and disappointments, has your faith failed? Talk with the Lord about your inner struggle, and ask for His help with your unbelief! Take your eyes off of your circumstances, and set them on your goal, stated so wonderfully in 2 Timothy 4:7!

10. What did Jesus do that was unheard of, even forbidden, in the Law? (v.41; see also Leviticus 13:44-46)

   Why did Jesus touch that man? (See Hebrews 2:17; 4:15)

   What was Jesus' relationship to the Law of Moses? To answer, read and summarize the following:

   Galatians 4:4:

   John 1:17:

   Matthew 5:17-48:

   Matthew 12:1-8:

11. How did Jesus instruct the cleansed leper? (v. 44; See also Leviticus 14:2,19-20)

12. Why did Jesus tell him not to tell anyone of his healing? Compare:

John 2:3-4:

Ecclesiastes 3:1:

13. What did the cleansed man do instead? (v. 45)

14. Now that Jesus Christ has revealed himself as Savior and Lord, and sits in glory at the right hand of the Father, what are we to do?
    See also:
    Mark 16:15

We have a great commission from our Lord!
Let us carry it out faithfully until His return for us!

Lesson Three: Mark 2

"For they loved the praise of men more than the praise of God."
- John 12:43

"Ye are of your father the devil, and the lusts of your father ye will do. He was a murderer from the beginning, and abode not in the truth, because there is no truth in him... And because I tell you the truth, ye believe me not. Which of you convinceth me of sin? And if I say the truth, why do ye not believe me? He that is of God heareth God's words: Ye therefore hear then not, because ye are not of God."
- John 8:44-47

"For [Pilate] knew that for envy they had delivered Him."
- Matthew 27:18

In chapter two of Mark's gospel, we begin to see the opposition of the scribers and Pharisees to Jesus, and apportions which would build, from criticism to vicious hatred, and would culminate in the death of our Lord Jesus on the cross.

The Pharisees, or "separated ones," held complete sway over the nation Israel after the Babylonian captivity. Because of their punctilious observance of the Law, the Pharisees had the admiration of the multitudes, and even under the Roman government were able to maintain their spiritual authority. Even though the Saducean High Priests were at the head of the Sanhedrin, the Pharisees' instructions were obeyed in all acts of public worship, prayers, and sacrifices. They completely controlled the public life of the nation, as the self-appointed determiners of right conduct, down to the minutest detail. Their devotion to the letter of the law in a thousand minute precepts, distinctions, and trifling instructions, had the whole life of the nation hemmed in on every side. Under the control of the Pharisees, the people had lost track of the fact that God had not given the law as and end in itself, but as a means to show a man's need for a Redeemer, who alone could deal with the sin in man's heart.

When the Redeemer came, bringing to life the underlying principles of the law, which God had intended, i.e. "I will have mercy, and not sacrifice,"[4] the Pharisitical system was shaken down to its foundation. And when Jesus performed His substantiating miracles, which even the Pharisees had to acknowledge were from God, their envy became furious. They realized that they were losing their grip on the people. As the Pharisees said among themselves after the raising of Lazarus, "You see that you are accomplishing nothing. Look, the world has done after Him!"[5]

Envy is a hideous sin – it truly is "rottenness of the bones."[6] Envy is prominent in every list of vile sins given in the New Testament, and closely associated with murder. Why? Because when one person envies another, there is almost no limit to what one might do, and indeed, you have murdered them in your heart. 1 John 3:15 says, "Whosoever hateth his brother is a murderer."

If you are tempted to envy someone today, think of the terrible sin of the scribes and Pharisees, and confess it to the Lord. Realize, dear fellow Christian, that God has a special place for you, and has allowed just the right circumstances in your life so that He might use you in His time. Your part is to be faithful and obedient and watch his plan unfold! Praise Him today!

Read Mark 2

Please **pray** for the help of the Holy Spirit before you answer the questions.

1. Describe the response to Jesus' teaching (v. 1-2).

    As always, what did Jesus do? (v.2; See also Mark 1:38; Luke 4:18; John 18:37)

2. What had Capernaum become to Jesus? (see Matthew 4:13, 9:1)

---

[4] Matthew 9:13, Hosea 6:6
[5] John 12:19
[6] Proverbs 14:30

Yet what did he say about that city? (Matthew 11:23-24)

3. What were the friends of the palsied man forced to do because of the crowd? (v.4)

Should a Christian ever grow weary of seeking an answer from God? Why or why not?
(See Luke 18:1; Ephesians 6:18; 1 Thessalonians 5:17)

To help support you answer, summarize the following verses:
    Genesis 32:24-30:

    1 Samuel 1:9-19:

    Nehemiah 1:1-11:

    Psalm 30:

    Daniel 9:16-23:

    Luke 11:5-10:

4. Which quality did these men demonstrate through their actions on behalf of their friend? (v.5)

Recount these other times when Jesus responded to outstanding faith in an individual:

    Matthew 15:21-28:

Luke 7:1-10:

How is your faith today? If need be, cry out to God with the man in Mark 9:24,
"Lord I believe; help thou mine unbelief."

5. What was Jesus' statement to the palsied man? (v.5)

   Describe these other times in scripture where we see the connection between sin and illness:

   John 5:5-8,14:

   1 Corinthians 11:29-30:

   James 5:15:

6. Describe the thoughts of the scribes. (v. 6-7)

   How were they wrong? (See Romans 9:5b; Revelation 19:16)

   How were they right? (See Job 14:4; Isaiah 43:25)

7. How did Jesus know what they were thinking? Use the following scriptures to answer:
   1 Samuel 16:7, Psalm 139:1-2, John 2:24-25, Hebrews 4:13:

   Therefore, how did Jesus vindicate himself? (v.10-12)

8. Whom did Jesus call in verse 14? (See also: Matthew 9:9)

What kind of person was he? (See also: Luke 18:10-13)

Yet how did he respond to the call of Jesus? (v. 14-15)

Is anyone too evil to be saved by Christ? (See also: Luke 23:39-43)

What was your lifestyle before Christ made a new person of you? Praise Him for His goodness and mercy!

9. The self-righteous Pharisees now had a major complain about Jesus, what was it? (v. 16).

   What was Jesus' reply? Summarize His scathing comment to them found in Matthew 21:31b:

10. The disciples of John were honestly puzzled by something. What was it? (v. 18)

11. Did God ever command fasting? (See Leviticus 16:29-34)

    What other kinds of occasions called for fasting?

    See the following Scriptures:

    2 Samuel 12:15-17:

    Esther 3:13; 4:3,14-16:

    Jonah 3:5-10:

    Joel 1:13-15; 2:12-18:

What did God have to say about Israel's fasting?

    Isaiah 58:3-7

    Jeremiah 14:12:

12. How had the Pharisees abused fasting? (See also: Luke 18:11-12)

    What was Jesus' comment about them? (See also: Matthew 6:16)

13. Give your explanation of the illustration of the bridegroom that Jesus gives in verses 19-20. For help, use the following scriptures where the illustration is developed further: Matthew 25:1,10,13; John 3:28-29; 2 Corinthians 11:2; Ephesians 5:31-32; Revelation 19:7-9.

14. What did Christ say about hanging on to old traditions, rituals, and ways of thinking in verses 21-22?
    Write these verses:

        Matthew 15:6b,9:

        Mark 7:8,9:

        2 Corinthians 5:17:

        Colossians 2:8:

Are you guilty of trusting in rituals and traditions to sustain your relationship with Christ? Or is every day a fresh opportunity to allow God to work unhindered?
Take to heart Isaiah 43:18-19: "Remember ye not the former things, neither consider the things of old. Behold, I will do a new thing; now it shall spring forth; shall ye not know it? I will even make a way in the wilderness and rivers in the desert."

15. The Pharisees had a new criticism of Jesus' disciples in verse 24. What was it?

    Was this really unlawful? Use Leviticus 23:22 and Deuteronomy 23:25 to support your answer.

    What had the Pharisees done in regard to the Sabbath? (See Matthew 23:4,24)

16. Which greatly revered patriarch did Jesus use to confront the Pharisees? (See also: 1 Samuel 21:1-6)
    What is the true purpose of the Sabbath? (v.27; Exodus 23:12)

17. Jesus made a very definite statement of who He was in verse 28. Who is He?

    Summarize similar statements found in the following verses:

    Acts 10:36:

    Romans 9:5

    Matthew 25:31:

Philippians 2:9-11:

1 Timothy 6:15:

Thank you Lord that you are Lord of all!
May You be Lord of our lives, as we submit ourselves to you!

Lesson Four: Mark 3

"And he goeth up into a mountain, and calleth unto Him who He would: and they came unto Him. And He ordained twelve, that they should be with Him, and that He might send them forth to preach, and to have power to heal sickness, and to cast out devils."
- Mark 3:13-15

"Ye have not chosen me, but I have chosen you, and ordained you, that ye should go and bring forth fruit, and that your fruit should remain..."
- John 15:6

"For ye see your calling brethren, how that not many wise men after the flesh, not many mighty, not many noble, are called: but God hath chosen the foolish things of the world to confound the wise; and God hath chosen the weak things of the world to confound the things which are might; and base things of the world, and things which are despised, hath God chose, yea, and things, which are not, to bring to naught things that are: that no flesh should glory in His presence."
- 1 Corinthians 1:26-29

The miraculous, Sprit-filled ministry of Jesus continues in chapter three, with the healing of the man with the withered hand. Because He boldly healed the man on the Sabbath, in the synagogue, a man who had been deliberately planted there by Jesus' enemies, the Pharisees and Herodians decided right then to destroy Him. Oh, the hardness of hearts of these men who knew they were losing their influence! The Law, which they so fervently stood for, was being fulfilled by Jesus, in the spirit, not in the letter! So now we see two opposing parties banding together in their envy and wickedness, to kill Him. Jesus prudently withdrew, because His time was not yet come.

Yet the multitudes continued to come to Jesus, so many in number that His life was endangered and He had to teach from a boat. The principle for us here is that Jesus did not remain defiantly in the middle of His enemies, nor surrounded by the pressing crowds; neither are we to tempt God with a lack of precaution for our physical bodies.

As this busy chapter continues we turn our focus to the selection and calling of the twelve apostles. Luke 6:12-13 enlightens us further:

> "And it came to pass in those days that He went out into a mountain to pray, and continued all night in prayer to God. And when it was day, He called unto Him His disciples, and of them He chose twelve, who He also named apostles."

Jesus had many more disciples, perhaps the 7- which are referred to in Luke 10. But He particularly ordained twelve men, for three purposes, as described in Mark 3:14-15. First, they were to be with Him. Their most important duty was to spend time in the presence of Jesus, to learn from Him, follow Him, to absorb His very nature into their innermost beings. The twelve were to sit at His feet in devotion, to learn to know Him and His Word. Literally abiding with Jesus was their preparation for ministry, just as we are to abide in Him. For without His personal presence and relationship, we can do nothing. Second, Jesus' purpose for them was to go forth and preach. We read elsewhere in Mark[7] that He sent them out two by two, as witnesses of all they had seen and heard from their master, preaching the gospel and bringing souls into the kingdom of God. We have the same commission. Third, Jesus gave them power, the Power of His Name, over sickness and Satan, for "greater is He that is in you than he that is in the world."[8] The power of the Holy Spirit is available to us as well. We need not be victimized by Satan's miserable afflictions! Is your desire to be a disciple of Christ? Spend time with Him, alone, that your devotional time will bear fruit and build the kingdom of God as you go forth in power.

God is still ordaining men and women to be His disciples today. Just as He chose the simple, working men, who would give a straightforward witness of the person and power of Christ, Jesus is not looking for brilliance and talent (not that He cannot use these qualities He Himself gave, when channeled in His direction). He looks for those who desire to serve Him with an honest heart, those who will offer all that they are and allow Christ to mold them into people of incredible value in the body of Christ. We offer ourselves as living sacrifices[9]; He does the perfecting, for indeed, "He makes all things beautiful in His time."[10]

---

[7] Mark 6:7
[8] 1 John 4:4
[9] Romans 12:1
[10] Ecclesiastes 3:11

Dana Kruckenberg Thompson

Read Mark 3

Please **pray** for the wisdom of the Holy Spirit as you answer the questions.

1. Where did the next confrontation with the Pharisees take place? (v. 1-2)

    What were the Pharisees watching for? (Psalm 64:3-5)

    Why?

    Did they care for the man with the withered hand? (See 1 Corinthians 13:4a)

    Did the Law forbid healing on the Sabbath? See Exodus 23:12

    Leviticus 23:1-3 to formulate your answer. Also, keep in mind Mark 2:28.

2. How did Jesus respond to the Pharisees? (v.3) Did He fear their reaction? (Proverbs 28:1).

    Are you fearful today? Fearful of what others think of you, or what they might say about you? Confess this to the Lord and realize that "God has not given us the Spirit of fear, but of power, and of love, and of sound mind." – 2 Timothy 1:7. In addition, meditate on Hebrews 13:6.

3. Jesus' question in v. 4 has a far-reaching implication for us. In your own words, describe what He is saying.

There is no middle ground!

Consider these Scriptures:

> Matthew 12:30

> James 4:17

*Have you been living in compromise, content with simply refraining from doing evil, but not actively going forth to do good?
Let Jesus' example set you on a right path!*

4. Why didn't the Pharisees have an answer?

5. Describe Jesus' emotions in verse 5.

   When else have we seen Him angered and grieved? (John 2:13-17)

   Have you ever felt this way?

   Using a New Testament Greek word study, look up "hardness". Compare this with what God said He would do for the Jews in Ezekiel 11:19-20 and 36:26-27.

6. Jesus did exactly as the Pharisees expected Him to. Why? (See 2 Timothy 2:13, Lamentations 3:22-23, 1 Thessalonians 5:24 & 1 Peter 4:19)

7. How did the Pharisees and Herodians proceed to profane the Sabbath themselves? (v.4-6)

Use Acts 2:22-23 to describe God's viewpoint of their actions.

8. What prudent action did Jesus take in verse 7? (See also: Luke 4:12)

   Describe Jesus' itinerary:

   Why did He have to get onto a small boat? (v. 8-10)

   Is your life having a far-reaching and widespread impact upon others for Christ?
   Seek the Lord daily, that is may be so!

9. Again we see the reaction of unclean spirits. What did they say about Christ?

   Did that make them believers? (See James 2:19b)

   When you witness, what do you say about Jesus?

10. Describe the calling of the disciples. (v. 13-15)

    What does Luke 6:12 tell us about Jesus' preparation for calling them?

    How much time do you spend in prayer before making major (or even minor) decisions? If Jesus spent all night in prayer, how much more should we, in our feebleness, spend?

11. Point out any outstanding characteristics of the disciples you notice in the account in Mark. Refer also to Luke 9:53-56 and Matthew 16:18.
    Who of the twelve apostles wrote books of the New Testament?

Which apostle(s) did Herod martyr? (Acts. 12:1-2)

12. Write these scriptures that refer to Judas:

    Psalm 41:9:

    John 6:70-71:

    John 12:4-6:

    Matthew 26:14-16:

    Acts 1:16-18:

13. Why did Jesus' relatives come to get Him? (v. 21)

    To this day, what do people say about a person who whole-heartedly and with singleness of purpose serves God?

14. What did the scribes have to say about Jesus? (v. 22)

    Give the gist of Jesus' reply to them in verses 22-27.

15. There is a dire warning in verses 28-30. Write it in your own words.

    What is the only hope of salvation for any man?

16. Jesus' family continued to call Him away. What was His answer to them? (v.33-35) Also refer to Luke 14:26, Romans 8:29 and Hebrews 2:11.

*Let us determine to be in the "new" family of Christ by doing His will.
Help us, Lord Jesus, to follow You, to count the cost,
and count the cost as nothing in comparison to knowing You!*

Lesson Five: Mark 4

> "Unto you it is given to know the mystery of the kingdom of God: but unto them that are without, all these things are done in parables: that seeing they may see and not perceive, and hearing they may hear, and not understand; lest at any time they should be converted, and their sins should be forgiven them."
> - Mark 4:11-12

> "It is a people that do err in their heart, and they have not known my ways…"
> - Psalm 95: 10

> "What manner of man is this, that even the wind and the sea obey Him?"
> - Mark 4:41

In Mark Chapter four, we have a parable within a parable: one or the people of Jesus' day, and one for us.

The parable was a very popular method of teaching in eastern cultures. It is a lengthy narrative drawn from nature or human circumstances in order to present a spiritual meaning. The hearer must catch the analogy in order to be instructed, as with a proverb. One must have "ears to hear." The multitudes were not capable of understanding, by reason of spiritual blindness, while the Pharisees and scribes were in blatant opposition to our Lord's every word and deed. Isaiah faced the same conditions in the people of Israel in the day of his ministry: their hearts were fat, their ears heavy, and their eyes shut[11]. That is ever the deceitfulness of sin! All desire or capacity for knowing the truth is taken away. And God is not mocked. Jesus' withholding the meaning of the parables from the multitudes was a divine judgment upon the unworthy.

As Jesus expounds the parable of the sower, we find four types of people who hear the gospel: those who allow the enemy to take it away from them immediately, those who accept the word with great excitement, but walk away from the Lord when affliction arises, those for whom the cares and riches of this world are of first importance--they just do not have time for the

---
[11] Isaiah 6:10

savior, and last, those who accept the Word believe it, live it, and bring others into the kingdom.

Are you a born-again Christian today? There is a parable for you here also, beyond that of receiving the gospel message. How is your reception of the whole counsel of God? Not just the promises and blessings, but the instruction, exhortation, and correction? The ears of many Christians are open to the wonderful and exciting aspects of the Word of God but closed to the convicting words of the Holy Spirit, which would require us to change our lives. Hardness of heart sets in, and our spiritual condition is little better than that of the Jews of Jesus' day, for to whom much has been given, of him shall much be required.[12] We have been given a tremendous amount of light!

As we consider the last verse of our chapter, where the disciples ask in total fear, "what manner of man is this that even the wind and the sea obey Him?" we may find some insight into our often poor reception of God's Word. We fail to truly realize who Jesus is. When we fail to put the principles of God's word into action in our lives, such as esteeming others above ourselves, being cheerful givers, submitting to our spouse, waiting for God's timing, accepting His will in a situation, or seeking His wisdom, we are not trusting Jesus! We are not trusting Him to know what we need, to cover us with the shadow of His wings, to have a perfect plan for us. We are absolutely oblivious to the fact that Jesus is the Man who stilled the storm with a word, who allows our faith in His Word to be tested, but never, *never* more than we can endure.

My trust was tested as I wrote this on November 24, 1987. A small earthquake shook the house at 5:16 a.m., rattling windows, shelves, and moving the floor. My husband was already on his way to work, leaving me responsible for four young children. At first, my trust got shaky, as any mother's would, at the thought of the ultimate tragedy: the loss of her children. Then I just told the Lord as I stood in a doorway and the children continued peacefully sleeping, "I know You can cover us." The earthquake ended. We must realize that these are the end times, and there will be more earthquakes, more serious ones. The Word of God makes that clear. [13]

---

[12] Luke 12:48
[13] Matthew 24:8

I, along with every other believer, now am left with the question, "Where is my faith?" In my own emergency preparedness measures (just as the disciples applied their sailing skills that stormy night) or in the One who shakes this earth as He wills--and also stills it?

Read Mark 4

Please ask for the guidance of the Holy Spirit before you answer the questions.

    1. Why did Jesus find it necessary to get into a ship? (v.1 and John 12:19)

    How does Christ draw men unto Him today?
    (John 3:14-15, 12:32-33; 1 Corinthians 12:3b)

    Give your testimony of accepting Christ.

    2. What was Jesus' teaching method?

    What is a parable? (See Psalm 78:2)

    3. Read the parable of the sower in verses 3-8.

    Why would this story be one that the people could receive?

  4. What is Jesus' challenge to them in verse 9?

> *Do you have "ears to hear" what is said to you in God's Word,*
> *in that you act upon that Word to grow in the Lord?*

Prepare to share a special experience with the group of God's Word to you.

5. What privilege did Jesus give to the disciples in verse 11? (See also: Matthew 13:11-12)

   Why was this so tremendous an honor? (See also: Matthew 13:17; 1 Corinthians 2:8-10,16; Colossians 1:26,27; Hebrews 11:13; I Peter 1:9-10)

6. How is prophecy fulfilled in this passage? (v.11-12) Also refer to Matthew 13:13-15 and Isaiah 6:9-10.

7. What shows you the importance of this parable? (v.13)

8. Explore instances in scripture of individuals who fit the categories described in this parable.

   Verse 15: see Mark 6:20; Matthew 14:3-9

   Verse 16&17: see John 6:57-66

   Verse 18-19: Luke 18:18-24; 1 Timothy 6:9-10

   Verse 20: Luke 11:28; John 8:31; Colossians 1:23; 1 John 2:24

   As a Christian, you have received the Word, and are in Christ! Now, how much fruit are you bearing: for the kingdom of God? (See John 15:1-5)

9. How does verse 21 show us what we are to do with the gospel? (See also Matthew 5:14-16)

   What is the source of light? (See 2 Samuel 22:29)

10. What does Jesus say about the truth of His Word in verse 22?

    Does He intend the mystery to be revealed? (See Matthew 10:26-27)

    The result: (See John 1:1-4; 1 Peter 1:11-12).

11. Why do we need to be careful of what we hear, according to verse 24? (Also see 1 John 4:1)

    With what measure shall we give out that which He have heard? (See Corinthians 9:6)

    What is the warning to those who are not diligent in hearing, keeping and sharing the Word? (v.25; 2 Samuel 22:27; Matthew 25:29-30)

12. Read the description Jesus gives of the kingdom of God in verse 26-29.

    Can anyone explain how the kingdom of God grows, any more that they can explain how rain comes forth? Is the growth of either caused by man's efforts? Write your opinion here.
    Who will be the reapers of the harvest of souls? (See Matthew 13:37-43)

13. As you look at the picture Jesus gives of the kingdom of God in verses 30-32, share from your current perspective how it has grown. (Also see Matthew 10:1,7; Matthew 28:19-20; Jude 14; Revelation 5:9-12)

14. Verses 35-41 contain such lessons for us! Read this passage carefully before answering the questions.

    What happened as they crossed the lake in their boat?

    Are you in a storm with troubles threatening to drown you? 'Where do you see the Lord in your situation?

15. What was Jesus doing when the storm commenced? (v.38)

    What does this show about Him? (See also Romans 15:33; Philippians 4:7)

16. Does God ever really sleep through our trials?

    Read and summarize Psalm 121

17. How did Jesus respond to their question and plea for help? (v.39)

    Write these scriptures:

    Job 38:8,11:

    Psalm 89:8-9:

Nahum 1:3-4a:

How will He respond to your cry?

18. Why did Jesus rebuke the disciples? (v.40; also see 2 Timothy 1:7)

What is right about the fear the men had in verse 41?
(Also refer to Psalm 33:8-9; Proverbs 1:7; Ecclesiastes 12:13; Jeremiah 32:39-40)

As we walk through our trials with the lord Jesus let us expect deliverance, keeping in mind Isaiah 46:9-11:
"I am God, and there is none else; I am God,
and there is none like me.
Declaring the end from the beginning, and from ancient times the things that are not yet done, saying, my counsel shall stand, and I will do all my pleasure: yea, I have spoken it, I will also bring it to pass; I have purposed it, I will also do it."

Lesson Six: Mark 5:1-20

"He is despised and rejected of men; a man of sorrows, and acquainted with grief: and we hid as it were, our faces from Him; He was despised, and we esteemed Him not."
- Isaiah 53:3

"He came unto His own, and His own received Him not."
- John 1:11

"And this is the condemnation, that light is come into the world, and men loved darkness rather than light, because their deeds were evil."
- John 3: 19

"If I had not done among them the works which none other man did, they had not had sin: but now have they both seen and hated both me and my Father."
- John 15:24

In one of the most arresting incidents in ministry of Jesus, we find Him confronted with utter human depravity in the land of the Gerasenes. He healed and restored the demoniac with a word, casting out legions of demons into a herd of swine. There is an important lesson for us here. Because this man worshipped and trusted Jesus, his condition was curable. But the truly depraved condition of mankind was demonstrated later on, in those who witnessed this deliverance. These men made it clear that they wanted nothing to do with Jesus, as they bade him, "Depart from our coasts!"

As it was at His birth when there was no room in the inn, it is today. Jesus is despised and rejected by willful sinners. Rather than acknowledge who He is, men would rather dwell with swine. As it was unlawful for the Jews of the area to raise pigs, it is unlawful today for men to employ themselves in the almost inconceivable forms of wickedness that we hear and read of daily. There is certainly no room for Jesus in the hearts of those who perform abortions (even on young girls), who produce child pornography, who indulge in extramarital "affairs", or drug trafficking. If one acknowledges the person of Christ, it will certainly mean the end of those lucrative "insider" deals, homosexuality, or backstabbing in the office.

When Jesus Christ comes into a life, He comes to cast out, and to clean out, any and all elements of a person's life which conflict with His character. And while we find it easy to point out vile sins such as those practiced by godless people, (just as the demoniac's condition was obviously of Satan) we perhaps need to review, from God's perspective, the sins that the Bible calls abhorrent: "unrighteousness, sexual immorality, wickedness, covetousness, maliciousness, full of envy, murder, strife, deceit, evil-mindedness; whispers, backbiters, haters of God, violent, proud, boasters, inventors of evil things, disobedient to parents, undiscerning, untrustworthy, unloving, unforgiving, unmerciful."[14] Notice how many of these sins are subtle, proceeding from a prideful heart in rebellion to God!

Many Christians, like the Gerasene citizens, can confess to wishing that Jesus, and His convicting Holy Spirit, would go away, rather than confess and repent of their besetting sin. They would rather keep their swine! We need not remain in a sinful condition today. There is help for our hearts! "If we confess our sins, He is faithful and just to forgive us our sins, and cleanse us from all unrighteousness."[15] As we carefully consider our chapter today, let us keep in mind what Jesus said: "A good man out of the good treasure of the heart brings forth good things: and an evil man out of the evil treasure brings forth evil things."[16] May our hearts be places in which Jesus is not only welcome, but pleased to be at home!

Read Mark 5:1-20

Please **pray** for the guidance of the Holy Spirit as you answer the questions.

1. Where did Jesus and the disciples arrive? (v. 1)

    Discuss the history of this region and its people.
    (Refer to Numbers 32: 1-7; 14-33)

    Were the Gadites in unity with the rest of the Israelites? Why or why not?

---

[14] Romans 1:29-31, NKJV
[15] 1 John 1:9
[16] Matthew 12:34-35

Contrast Psalm 133:1 and Proverbs 6:19b

What caused them to desire the area east of Jordan?

Who does this remind you of? (Genesis 13:10-11)

How are we to judge situations and make decisions? Answer based on the following:

Proverbs 1, 2:6-11:

Ecclesiastes 2:5:

John 7:24:

1 Corinthians 2:15-16:

Ephesians 5:17:

How had the Gadarenes degenerated by the time of Jesus? (v:11)

Discuss the progression of sin based on James 1:13-15:

2. Describe the man who came to meet Jesus (v. 2-5).

*Perhaps you know of someone in this condition today.
Ask the Lord for spiritual discernment that you might know how to pray,
and commit to pray for this person daily this week.
The Lord may reveal to you that you have the gift described in 1
Corinthians 12:10!*

3. What did the man do? (v.6)

   Write these scriptures on worship:

      Psalm 95:6:

      Psalm 100:4:

      Psalm 103:1:

      Luke 4:8:

      John 4:23-24:

      Acts 2:4:

   What must even the demons do at last?
   (Review Philippians 2:9-11; James 2:19)

4. What did the demon have to say in verse 7?

   Use these verses to describe who Jesus is:

      Isaiah 7:14:

Isaiah 9:6:

Isaiah 59:20:

Daniel 9:24-25:

John 1:1:

John 1:29:

Romans 9:5:

1 Timothy 2:3:

Titus 3:6:

James 2:1:

1 John 5:20:

Revelation 15:3:

Revelation 17:14:

Who is Jesus to you?

5. How was the casting out of the demon accomplished? (v. 8)

Using these verses, explore the power of a word from God:
Genesis 1:3-6:

Matthew 26:53:

Hebrews 11:3:

James 1:18:

1 Peter 1:23:

6. Why was the demon called "Legion"?

   What was their request? (v. 10)

   Why? (See Matthew 12:43-45 for some insight)

7. Should the Gadarenes have been raising pigs? Why or why not? (Refer to Leviticus 11:7-8; Deuteronomy 14:8)

   How can we know that there were Jews in this region?
   (See Matthew 10:5-6, 15:24)

8. After Jesus gave permission to the unclean spirits to enter the swine, what did the herd do? (v.13)

9. Think carefully: did Jesus destroy the pigs? (See John 10:10)

If so, had He the right? Why or why not?

(See Psalm 50:10; Mark 11:12-14; 2 Peter 3:10)

10. As a child of God, what hope do you have based on 2 Peter 3:11-13?

What does this mean to you?

11. What sight did the townspeople whom the herdsmen alerted see when they arrived? (v.15)

What emotion did they express?

In your opinion, what did they fear?

Yet, Jesus was fulfilling His commission from the rather found in 1John 3:8b.

12. Should we fear God and His works?

Summarize the following:

Deuteronomy 10:20-21:

Psalm 4:4:

Psalm 34:7-11:

Proverbs 14:26-27:

Ecclesiastes 12:13:

2 Corinthians 7:1:

Philippians 2:12:

How would you describe your fear of God?

13. How did the townspeople respond to this miracle of deliverance? (v.17)

    Why? (Refer to John 3:19)

14. What did Jesus do, therefore, in verse 18?

    How is this characteristic of Him? (See Luke 10:10-11; Revelation 3:20)

    He gives each one the choice - receive or reject!

15. What did the delivered man desire to do? (v.18)

    However, what better thing did the Lord have for him to do? (v.19-20)

16. Often, as we seek a ministry, we feel that we are well-suited or even just desire a certain calling. But the Lord often has a surprise for us! Describe how this may have come to pass in your life as God blessed you by revealing His perfect will to you:

Let us worship our Lord today, acknowledge who He is, and prepare our hearts and homes to receive Him. "Have thine own way, Lord, have thine own way."

Lesson Seven: Mark 5:21-43

> "Fear not: believe only, and she shall be made whole."
> - Luke 8:50

> "...God, who quickens the dead, and calleth those things that be not as though they were."
> - Romans 4:17

> "Faith is the substance of things hoped for, the evidence of things not seen."
> - Hebrews 11:1

> "Your faith should not stand in the wisdom of men, but in the power of God."
> - 1 Corinthians 2:5

We see in the latter half of our chapter, two touching examples of faith in the power of the Lord Jesus Christ, which speak to us twenty centuries later just as strongly as on the day they took place.

Jesus had been warmly and tumultuously received by the people on His arrival from Decapolis - quite in contrast with the hostile send-off He had just experienced. I see the beautiful grace and mercy of God here for His servants. How often have we returned saddened by the rejection of godless people to find a warm welcome in the arms of Christian brothers and sisters? Praise Him!

In the midst of the needy, noisy throng came Jairus, an elder of the synagogue desperately entreating Jesus for the life of his twelve-year-old daughter. "I pray thee, come and lay thy hands on her, that she may be healed, and she shall live."[17] Jesus always responded to such true and intense faith; His response was to immediately go with Jairus. It is very clear that the faith of Jairus was well pleasing to God.

Meanwhile, another faith-filled individual came to Jesus in her hour of desperation, only surreptitiously, as a societal outcast. This woman had hemorrhaged for twelve years (ironically, the same number of years as the

---
[17] Mark 5:23

life of the dying girl!) and, by law, was not to be touched by anyone. She had undoubtedly been divorced by her husband for her uncleanness, was considered a vile sinner. As such, could not enter the court of women in the synagogue or temple, would no longer have access to her children, and she had been taken advantage of by her physicians. She was truly a pathetic soul. But as her life issued from her, she had one last desperate hope: "If I may but touch His garment, I shall be whole."[18] By no direct action of the Lord's, yet by the power of the Holy Spirit, she was healed, immediately and completely! In 1980, it was this scripture that encouraged me to pray in faith for healing of a similar (however, much less lengthy) affliction. God healed me also and it has never recurred. As Ecclesiastes 3:14 says, "Whatsoever God doeth, it shall be forever: nothing can be put to it, nor anything taken from it."

Then, the bad news came to Jairus at that very moment: his daughter was dead - there was no need to vex the Master any further. But Jesus said to Jairus five words, which if we would appropriate, would change our lives: "Be not afraid, only believe."[19] And Jairus did, hoping against hope. We never read of one shred of unbelief in this man! As we rejoice in the restoration of the girl to her parents, we see that while the power was God's, faith was the instrument!

Do you believe God today that he can bring deliverance from your trial, give you guidance, or heal your physical affliction? As Christians, we need to take seriously Hebrews 11:6: "Without faith it is impossible to please Him: for He that comes to God must believe that He is and that He is a rewarder of them that diligently seek Him."

Read Mark 5:21-43

Please **pray** for the guidance of the Holy Spirit as you answer the following questions.

1. How was Jesus received when He returned from Decapolis?

---

[18] Matthew 9:21
[19] Mark 5:36

What realistic, characteristic, observation did Jesus make later about these crowds? (Also refer to John 4:48 & 6:26)

Why are you following Christ?

What are the reasons we should be following Christ? List the reasons found in the following verses:

John 6:65:

1 Corinthians 12:3b:

John 20:31:

Philippians 2:15:

2. Who came to Jesus in the midst of the crowd? (v.22)

Briefly recount the stories of these others who came to Jesus under similar circumstances:

Matthew 8:5-13:

Matthew 15:21-28:
Which characteristic did these three people have in common?

How do these three people represent the entire human race?
(You may use your Bible dictionary. Also refer to Genesis 10:1-3 & 21)

Share, if you choose, the time when you went to Jesus in faith in your deepest need.

3. As Jesus followed Jairus, who else approached? (v.25-26)

   Describe her.

   What made her condition so pitiful? Summarize in your own words. Refer to Leviticus 15:25-27,31

4. Despite her being an outcast, what did she determine to do when she heard of Jesus? (v.27-28)

   What intense need in your life caused you to come to Jesus?

   What had you heard that He could do for you?

5. Describe her miracle. (v. 29)

   Did Jesus take any direct action? Nevertheless, what took place? (v.30a) (See these verses: Mark 1:10, Luke 4:1, John 3:34b)

6. How did the disciples misunderstand the question that Jesus asked in verse 30?   (see v.31)

   Give your opinion: Did Jesus actually not know who touched him?

   Write these verses to support or challenge your answer:

1 Kings 8:39:

Job 23:10 & 31:4:

Jeremiah 23:24:

Hebrews 4:13:

7. Why then might Jesus have asked her to come forward?
   What are we told to do when God does a mighty work in our lives?
   (Refer to Acts 22:15; 1 Chronicles 16:23-24; Psalm 68:11)

Give a possible reason why the woman was fearful of coming forward (Refer to the scriptures in question three).

8. How did Jesus commend her? (v.34)

Pray to the Lord for a faith that is pleasing to Him!

9. What message came to Jairus at that moment? (v.35)

Describe the emotions that would have gone through the heart of this father.

How did Jesus calm him? (v.36; John 11:40)

What words of comfort do we find in scripture for times of tragedy?

Psalm 23:4:

Psalm 138:3,8:

John 11: 25:

1 Thessalonians 4:13-18:

10. Who only were allowed to come with Jesus and Jairus? (v.37) Cite these similar incidents: Matthew 17:1,2 Matthew 26:36,37

   Is there a scriptural precedent for selecting certain individuals in the church today for special ministry? See Acts 13:2-3 to formulate your answer.

11. What was the scene Jesus encountered at Jairus' house? (v.38) Use these scriptures for an understanding of Jewish mourning:

   2 Samuel 1:11-12:

   Esther 4:1:

   Jeremiah 10:17-18:

12. What shocking, seemingly ludicrous, statement did Jesus make to the mourners in verse 39?

   Is it possible that a part of her being *was* only sleeping? (See 1Samuel 30:12; Job 32:8; Psalm 31:5; Proverbs 20: 27; 1 Thessalonians 5:23)

13. Tell the instructions that the girl received from Jesus, and her action.

Did she comply?

14. How did Jesus show His constant compassion and concern for the physical need of this precious lamb? (v.43)

Lord Jesus, we thank you for this story, which shows us so vividly the compassion you have for every family, and how you desire to meet the need of each one. Praise You, Lord!

Lesson Eight: Mark 6:1-29

> "And He could there do no mighty work ... and He marveled because of their unbelief."
> - Mark 6:5-6

> "And whoever will not receive you, nor hear you, when you depart from there, shake off the dust under your feet as a testimony against them. Assuredly, I say to you, it will be more tolerable for Sodom and Gomorrah in the day of judgment than for that city."
> - Mark 6:11

> "Because sentence against an evil work is not executed speedily, therefore the heart of the sons of men is fully set in them to do evil."
> - Ecclesiastes 8:11

> "The fear of man brings a snare."
> - Proverbs 29:25

In the Gospel of Mark we have seen Jesus Christ, the Lord of Glory, God Omnipotent, raise the dead, cast out demons, and heal hundreds. Yet, this same God who spoke the world into existence, and who told the raging sea, "Be muzzled", found His hands tied in His hometown of Nazareth! He could not do any mighty works there at all. Is there a limit to omnipotence? Is there anything Jesus cannot do? This chapter of Mark shows us plainly that there is: Jesus cannot do a miraculous work in the life of someone who refuses to believe in His Name! Faith is the key that unlocks the power of God. Perhaps an afflicted individual does not know Christ and therefore does not pray for healing. Yet God may heal that person in response to the faith-filled prayers of believers, that He may be glorified, and that person then be saved. But when an entire community sets its face against Jesus in stonehearted unbelief, He can "do no mighty work". You see, as we are told in Acts 4:16, it is "through faith in His Name", that Jesus heals, delivers, and saves. Our God who reserves to Himself absolute control over this universe, over the sun, moon, stars, and all of life, will not invade the strongest bastion of all - the human heart. It must be given to Him freely, in faith. And as the apostles were sent out by twos (v.7-11) they were told only to abide in the homes of believers, and to shake the dust off their feet against those who rejected Christ.

The second part of our lesson shows us the unutterable wickedness (and cowardice) of Herod the Tetrarch of Galilee and his court. John the Baptist, whom Jesus described as "a burning and a shining light," [20]was being that light in the court of Herod. John uncompromisingly spoke the truth to the jaded monarch, as we should too, with all the boldness that knowing Christ gives us. Herod heard him gladly, until John confronted him about his personal sin. Ministries are often tolerated by ungodly people until the spotlight is turned onto the blackness of the sin in their lives! Then begins persecution.

Herod not only committed adultery with Herodias, but incest, for she was also a near relation. Herod imprisoned John, but it was the seething hatred of Herodias that had John beheaded finally, through the lewd dancing of her own daughter.

The bold and truthful witness for Christ will experience alienation from friends and family, persecution from unbelievers and relentless (though sometimes subtle) attacks from the devil. Jesus told us so! Read John 17:33: "In the world you shall have tribulation," and take to heart the remainder of the verse: "But be of good cheer; I have overcome the world".

Read Mark 6:1-29

Please **pray** for the help of the Holy Spirit as you answer the questions.

1. Where was Jesus' "own country"? (See also Matthew 2:23; Luke 4:16)

    What further definition do we find of the term "Nazarene"?
    (See Numbers 6:2-8)

    How might this apply to Jesus in a spiritual sense?
    (See Hebrews 7: 26)

---

[20] John 5:35

2. What was said of Jesus by his hometown people? (v.2-3)
   (For amplification, see Luke 4:16-24)

   How did Jesus identify Himself there? (Luke 4:18-21; Isaiah 61:1-2)

3. Give your opinion: Why were the Nazarenes so offended by Jesus?

How was this prophesied? Isaiah 53:1-3

4. Read Luke 4:28-30. How infuriated did the townspeople become?

   Has anyone ever been infuriated by your witness?

5. Witnessing to and exhorting family and childhood acquaintances is very, very difficult! Why? (See v. 4)

6. In verses 5 & 6, what was the extent of the opposition Jesus found in Nazareth? (See Isaiah 59:1-2)

Write these verses on unbelief:

   Psalm 95:8-11:

   Isaiah 7:9:

   John 1: 10-11:

   John 3:18:

John 8:24:

Acts 13:40-41:

Romans 14:23b:

2 Timothy 2:13:

Titus 1:15:

Revelation 21:8:

Are you in a state of unbelief today? If so, confess it to the Lord as sin!

7. What was the commission Jesus gave to the disciples? (v.7)

　How were they to travel? (v.8-10)

　　What were they to do when they encountered unbelief?
　　(v.11; Hebrews 10:31)

8. Did the disciples meet with success? (v.12-13)
　 (See Luke 10:17 for the outcome of the ministry of all of Jesus' disciples.)

Share with the group the joyous results of any outreach ministry you have participated in.

9. What did Herod hear about Jesus? (v.14-15; Matthew 16:13-14)
What did Herod think? Why? (Refer to Job 15:21; Proverbs 28:1)

   See these examples: John 8:9 Psalm 32:2-4

10. Why had Herod put John in prison? (v.17-18; 2 Timothy 4:2)

   What does God say?

   Leviticus 18:16:

   Leviticus 20:21:

   Hebrews 13: 4:

11. Why couldn't Herodias have John killed? (v.19)

   What had Herod's attitude been towards John? (v.20; Matthew 15:7-8)

12. Describe Herod's birthday party. (v.21-22)

   How did lecherous King Herod show himself to be a fool?
   (v.23; Ecclesiastes 5:2; Romans 1:28-29)

13. What did the girl request as her reward? (v.25)

   Why did Herod go through with it? (Refer to Proverbs 29:25; Luke 16:15; John 5:44; James 1:8)

14. Describe the end of John the Baptist's life. (v.27-29)

    What had been prophesied of him in Luke 1:17? Compare Matthew 17:11-13.

    How had Jesus described him? (See Matthew 11: 7-15)

Lord, we pray that we might be faithful to you in word and deed, no matter what consequences we might face in this life! May we end our days with a glorious testimony for you, and hear these words, "Well done, good and faithful servant: enter into the joy of the Lord."

Lesson Nine: Mark 6:30-56

"Oh that men would praise the Lord for His goodness, and for His wonderful works to the children of men! For He satisfies the longing soul, and fills the hungry soul with goodness."
- Psalm 107:8-9

"Be anxious for nothing; but in everything by prayer and supplication with thanksgiving let your requests be made known unto God."
- Philippians 4:6

"My God shall supply all your needs according to His riches and glory by Christ Jesus."
- Philippians 4:19

"Be of good cheer: it is I; be not afraid."
- Mark 6:50

In the only miracle recorded in all four gospels, we see a marvelous act of creation – the feeding of the five thousand. Only the Creator of all things could feed such a multitude from a meager provision of five loaves and two fishes brought by a young lad.

At the end of a long day of ministry, the disciples became concerned that the people were in a desert region with no place to purchase food. Jesus had compassion on the as well. But Luke 9:13 gives us a picture of the challenge presented to His disciples: "Give ye them something to eat." John 6:7 shows Philip's exasperation as he said of their small treasury, "200 pennyworth (or 28 dollars' worth) of bread is not sufficient for them, that every one of them may take a little." Of course, Jesus knew what He would do, and that all would be fed to the full, with twelve baskets of food to spare!

When Jesus asks us to do work for Him, we need never doubt that He will supply all that is needed to accomplish His will. The fact of the matter is, that Jesus through the power of the Holy Spirit, is actually the one who does the work! all we bring with us may be just a prayerful, willing, and obedient heart, little more that the lad's five loaves and two fishes. Think of the most challenging thing the Lords has ever asked of you. Was He not there all the time? Did He not give you the supernatural ability and eloquence, to the point, perhaps, that you would hardly have recognized yourself? It is only when we confess our utter spiritual bankruptcy that we become fit for the Master's use, and we enjoy the privilege of participating in miracles!

Once again, however, the Scripture reminds us of the frailty of the hearts of even the closest of Jesus' followers. That very evening after Jesus had sent his disciples to the other side of the lake that He might spend some time in prayer, He appeared to them, walking upon the sea. The men did not even recognize Jesus and thought He was a ghost. When their Lord identified himself and calmed the wind, "they were so amazed in themselves beyond measure, and wondered." Verse 52 is very direct and convicting, "For they considered not the miracle of the loaves: for their heart was hardened." The Holy Spirit makes it plain that even a temporary lapse of faith is unbelief, which is sin. Let us pray not only that our faith may not fail, but as we are called upon, that we may stand ready to strengthen our brethren also.[21]

As our chapter closes, we see that Jesus carried on His miraculous healing ministry to the waiting multitudes and so He continues to do so today, through His servants. The question for us is this: "Is my faith such that I will be able to have a part in the mighty works of God, or will hardness of heart render me useless?"

Read Mark 6:1-29

Please **pray** for the help of the Holy Spirit as you answer the questions.

1. What did the apostles do when they met with Jesus? (v. 30)

Which deeds had they been able to accomplish?
(Refer to Luke 10:17; Matthew 10:8)

What have you to report to Jesus?
How have you ministered in His name?

---

[21] Luke 22:32

2. When we are busy in ministry, what do we often forget, that Jesus counseled His disciples to do in verse 31?

    Write these Scriptures on setting aside time to be with Jesus:

    Psalm 4:4:

    Psalm 23:2:

    Psalm 63:6:

    Psalm 91:1-2:

    Matthew 11:28-30:

    Luke 10:38-42:

    Mark 1:35:

3. Yet, what did the people do? (v. 33)

    Was Jesus aggravated by them?

    How did He see them? (v.34)

    How was this prophesied? (Isaiah 54:13)

    Why did the common people not have shepherds?

Use the following Scriptures to answer:

Matthew 15:7-14:

Matthew 23:2-51; 13-15:

4. Write these verses describing our Lord:

Isaiah 40:11:

John 10:14-15 & 27-28:

Hebrews 13:20:

1 Peter 5:4:

5. What did the disciples bring to Jesus' attention in verse 36?

What did Jesus tell them to do? (v. 37)

Write their reply in these passages:

John 6:7-9:

Mark 6:37:

Give your opinion: What was the disciples' spiritual condition at this point?

Describe a time in your walk with the Lord when you have told Him that what He asked you was impossible:

Reflect on these verses: John 15:5b (last phrase) and Luke 1:37

6. What provision was there to offer the Lord? (v.38)

Can we really bring anything of value to the Lord?
Write the answer found in each of the following passages:

Romans 3:10,23:

Psalm 51:16-17:

Mark 12:33

Psalm 116:12-13:

What did the apostle Paul have to offer Christ?
Write the answer found in each of the following passages:
Acts 22:19-21:

Acts 26:9-19:

1 Corinthians 15:8-9:

Philippians 3:4-7:

7. How did Jesus arrange the people? (v.39-40; Refer also to 1

Corinthians 14:40)

8. How did Jesus multiply the food? (v. 41-42)

   What is the example Jesus set for us? (Refer to John 6:11; Psalm 106:1; Ephesians 5:20; 1 Thessalonians 5:18)

9. What was left over? What was to be done with the extra? (Also see John 6:12-13)

   What do you do with your leftover or extra food?
   What would God have you do?

10. Where did Jesus send the disciples? (v.45)

    What did he do himself? (v. 46)

    Why was this needful?

    Use the following verses to answer:
    John 6:14-15:

    John 18:36:

11. What happened to the disciples as they were out on the sea? (v. 48)

    Who did they think Jesus was? (v.49)
    Describe another time when this happened. (See Luke 24:36-43)

12. How does Jesus reassure us in times of fear?
    Answer based on the following Scriptures:

    Exodus 14:13-14:

    Psalm 23:4:

    Isaiah 51:12-13:

    2 Timothy 1:7:

    Hebrews 13:5-8:

13. Matthew 14:28-31 gives us the story of Peter's rejection. Recount it.

    Give your opinion: Did Peter have a well-founded faith?
    Why or why not?

14. How does the Lord see the attitude of the disciples? (v. 51-52)

    Write these other verses that describe the attitude of the flesh:

    Jeremiah 17:9:

    Romans 8:7-8:

    Hebrews 3:12-13:

*Do you find yourself in this spiritual condition today?
Confess it to Christ right away!*

15. Describe what happened in the land of Gennesaret, and the power of Jesus. (v. 53-56)

*We thank you, O Lord, for Your mighty works of healing
that we read of in Your Word.
We praise You that your power is present with us
to heal us today, as well!*

Lesson Ten: Mark 7

> "In vain do they worship me, teaching for doctrines the commandments of men."
>
> - Mark 7:7

> "The Lord said, for as much as this people draw near me with their mouth and with their lips do honor me, but have removed their heart far from me, and their fear toward me is taught by the precept of men."
>
> - Isaiah 29:13

> "There is nothing from without a man, that entering into him can defile him: but the things which come out of him, those are they that defile the man."
>
> - Mark 7: 15

> "Verily I say unto you, I have not found so great faith, no, not in Israel."
>
> - Matthew 8:10

As we saw in our last study, Jesus' reputation had grown tremendously, even reaching to the court of King Herod. Accordingly, a delegation of Pharisees and scribes was sent down from Jerusalem to spy on Jesus and His disciples, looking to find fault. And, of course, they did find fault in the fact that the disciples did not do the numerous prescribed ceremonial washings of the Pharisees and their followers. This was not a matter of personal hygiene, but of minute, unnecessary regulations. In this head-on confrontation with these leaders Jesus exposed them for what they were: hypocrites!

What was hypocritical about these men and their trifling observances? The hypocrisy lay in the fact that their entire religion consisted of keeping rules for external performance while having no actual personal relationship with God at all. Jesus and Isaiah said the same thing: "This people honor me with their lips, but their heart is far from me."

Do not think that "Pharisaism" (or the worship of external forms) rather than God) ended with the Pharisees! Christians can find themselves trapped in rigid requirements of religion, such as dressing a certain way, and many other "do's and don'ts" which their leaders may press upon them which have nothing whatever to do with God and His word. Sometimes a group's activities are dominated by an extreme and out-of-context interpretation of one scripture verse - and a religion of externals is perpetuated and justified.

The Pharisees, however, were guilty of an even greater sin: they had rejected the actual word of God in order to obey (and teach) their own traditions. They claimed that their traditions were orally handed down from Moses to Joshua, from Joshua to the elders, and from the elders to prophets, and therefore were valid. But there is no proof whatsoever of this. Their traditions arose during the period of time between the two testaments, when the scribes and Pharisees attempted to keep the Jewish way of life and religion alive. Unfortunately, what began as a noble thing became an end in itself, to the point of exclusion and even contradiction of the word of God itself, as Jesus points out in regard to the fifth commandment. Now here is one rule you may *always* rely upon: If any statement contradicts the Bible, it is not of God. For Psalm 138:2 tells us, "Thou hast magnified thy word above all thy Name." Not only did the Pharisees ignore the written word of God, but they led others down the same path, heaping to themselves damnation.

Externals cannot save nor defile - the condition of the heart is what Jesus addresses. Whereas we see in the scribes and Pharisees hearts full of pride, blasphemy, and hatred, we see in the Syrophenician woman, a Gentile, a heart full of faith. That faith (and persistence!) were rewarded with the deliverance of her daughter. Aptly, Hebrews 11:6 says, "He that comes to God must believe that He is, and that He is a rewarder of them that diligently seek Him!"

Read Mark 7

Please **pray** for the guidance of the Holy Spirit as you answer the questions.

1. Who came from Jerusalem to see Jesus? Why? Use these scriptures to find the answer:

    Mark 3:1-2:

Luke 11:54:

Galatians 2:4:

2. What fault did the Pharisees find with Jesus' disciples? (v. 2,5)

    Describe their tradition in regard to washing. (v.3-4)

    Was this a matter of cleanliness?

    What did the law of Moses have to say in regard to cleansing?
    Leviticus 22:5-6:

    Leviticus 14:2-9:

    Deuteronomy 23:10:

    Leviticus 17:15:

    Were the Pharisees, then, acting in accordance with the Law in their constant washings?

3. What did Jesus say was at the heart of their behavior? (v.6; Isaiah 29:13; Titus 1:14-16)

4. How were the Pharisees teaching service to God? (v.7,8)

    Matthew 23:4:

For us: Colossians 2:20-22:

What are the great commandments of the Law that Jesus said we must obey? (See Matthew 22:36-40)

What is the great commandment of the New Covenant?

John 13:34-35:

John 15:12:

5. Read verses 9-13. How had the Pharisees and scribes managed to circumvent the law in regard to the fifth commandment? (See also Exodus 21:17)

What is a Christian's duty to his family? (See 1 Timothy 5:8)

6. Discuss the Pharisees' giving:

Matthew 6:2:

Luke 21:1-4:

Matthew 23:23:

How are we to give to the Lord?

Matthew 6:4:

1 Corinthians 16:2:

2 Corinthians 8:12:

2 Corinthians 9:6-7:

7. What defiles a man? (v.15; Romans 14:17)

8. From reading verses 18-23, give Jesus' explanation of the above passage.

   Also see these verses:

   1 Corinthians 8:8:

   1 Timothy 4:4:

   Titus 1:15:

Are you guilty of any of these sins?
Confess them to the Lord today, and be cleansed!

9. Where did Jesus go next?

   What was prophesied of Tyre? (See Ezekiel 28:1-8 &17-19)

   Yet, what had Jesus to say about them in contrast to the Jews' unbelief? (See Luke 10:13-14; 12:48b)

10. Who came to Jesus there? (v.25-26)

    How was her request proof that faith in Christ was present in that region?

    (For further comment from Jesus on the faith of Gentiles, see Matthew 8:10-12)

11. What was the Syrophenecian woman's request? (v.26)

    How did Jesus reply? (v.27)

    Give your opinion: Was this cruel? Why or why not?

12. Who were "the children"? Read corresponding passage, Matthew 15:21-28 to help you answer, as well as Romans 2:10; 9:4-5.

13. Did the woman give up?

    What does her answer in verse 28 say about her character?

    Pray *for more humility and self-effacement in your relationship with Christ!*

14. Who was brought to Jesus in Decapolis? (v.32)

    How did Jesus heal him? (v.33-34)

Did Jesus use the same method for healing every time?

What do the scriptures have to say about expecting God to use the same methods and tactics to accomplish His purposes?

Joshua 6:12-16,20:

1 Samuel 14:6b:

2 Chronicles 14:11:

Isaiah 43:18-19:

Psalm 115:3:

Daniel 4:35:

Will you take some time today to marvel at the power of Christ released by faith, and worship Him?

For your personal worship time, **read Isaiah 40**.

*We thank you, O Lord, for who you are!
May we never limit you by our finite understanding!*

Lesson Eleven: Mark 8

> "An evil and adulterous generation seeketh after a sign: and there shall no sign be given to it, but the sign of the prophet Jonah. For as Jonah was three days and three nights in the whale's belly, so shall the Son of Man be three days and three nights in the heart of the earth."
>
> - Matthew 12:39-40

> "If any man will come after me, let him deny himself, and take up his cross, and follow me."
>
> - Matthew 16:24

> "But whom say ye that I am? Thou art the Christ, the Son of the living God."
>
> - Matthew 16:15-16

Our chapter begins with a miracle born of our Lord's compassion for the multitudes: the feeding of four thousand with only seven loaves and a few fish. The people had been with Jesus three days, attending to His teaching and their provisions had been spent. One cannot help but think of the times in our lives when our provisions have been all used up - spiritually, emotionally, and physically - and at this point, the Lord's miraculous supply of all our needs becomes available for the asking! "My God shall supply all your needs according to His riches in glory by Christ Jesus."[22]

The Pharisees then came to Jesus, seeking a sign, some display from the heavens that would verify His claims. But Jesus would not cater to their request, because their motives were impure, wicked, and the product of unbelief. Even if the Lord had produced fire from heaven, these men would not have believed. As He wisely stated in the parable of Lazarus and the rich man[23], rebellious men would not believe, even if a dead man came back from hell to testify to the danger of their souls! So the Savior warned His disciples of the leaven, or creeping insidious evil, of the Pharisees and Herod.

---

[22] Philippians 4:19
[23] Luke 16:31

Once again, however, we see doubt and puzzlement among the disciples, who thought Jesus was talking about literal bread. Thrilling, inspiring, and incomparable as it must have been to be one of Christ's disciples, I cannot help but thank God that I have his entire Word to tell me that Jesus Christ is Lord, God who came in the flesh, to die for me, and for the sin of the whole world! These men had to learn Jesus "from scratch", and I know with certainty that anyone of us would have stumbled along just as badly as they did, and possibly worse! Each one of us can confess to many times when we have stumbled at the written word, so we mustn't look askance at the original disciples. For a disciple is, in the Greek, "a learner", as all followers of Christ should be.

Even though Peter was later rebuked by Jesus for his complete misunderstanding of Christ's reason for coming to this earth, we see that he, and the rest of the disciples, had gotten hold of the most important truth, that Jesus is the Christ, the Son of the living God. Let a person grasp that fact, and ask Him for salvation, and Jesus Christ will reveal Himself in all His glory, to perform the greatest miracle of all - the bringing forth of new life from the dead!

Read Mark 8

Please **pray** for the guidance of the Holy Spirit before you answer the questions.

1. Why had the multitude been with Jesus for three days? (See Mark 6:34)

    In both passages, how did Jesus regard the people?

    Write these scriptures on the compassion of God:

    1 Chronicles 16:34:

    Psalm 30:5:

THE GOSPEL ACCORDING TO MARK: A Walk in the Word

    Read Psalm 103:3-17. Which of the verses meant the most to you?
    Read Psalm 85:10. Whom might this describe?

2. How many were fed? (v.9)

    What was left over?

    What do these verses say about God's provision?

        Psalm 104:10-14:

        Psalm 145:15-16:

What can you do to help a needy person know the goodness of the Lord?
*How can you **personally** become involved?*

3. What did the Pharisees want from Jesus? (v. 11)

    Why might they desire a sign to substantiate Jesus' claims?
    (See Exodus 9:23; 1 Samuel 7:8-10; 1 Kings 18:36-38)

4. What was the condition of these men's hearts?
   (See Matthew 12:39a)

    Give your opinion: Would they really have believed?

    Did Jesus feel the need to give them a sign? (v.12)

    Why not? (John 2:23-25)

5. According to Matthew 12:39-41 and John 2:18-21, what would be the only sign they would see from Him?
   Did the Jews even believe this sign? (See Matthew 28:1-15)

6. Read verses 14-20 carefully. What was Jesus' warning to His disciples? (v. 15)

   What was the leaven of the Pharisees and Sadducees? (Also see Matthew 16:12; Mark 12:18; Luke 12:1)

   What was the leaven of Herod? (Matthew 14:3-10, 22:16-21)

7. What caused the disciples to get confused? (v.14-16)

   How did Jesus correct them? (v.17-21)

   What was the "heart problem" that He found in them?

   Which "heart problem" plagues your walk with the Lord?

8. Describe the healing of the blind man. (v. 23-25)

   How might this parallel the believer's growth in the Lord?

9. Who did the people say Jesus was? (v.28; Matthew 16:14)

   Why might they think this way? (See Malachi 4:5-6; Luke 1:13-17;

Matthew 17:11-13)

10. Who did Peter say that He was? (Matthew 16:16; John 6:68-69) How did he know this? (Matthew 16:17)

    What is the only way a man can acknowledge Jesus? Answer based on the following Scriptures:

    John 6:44:

    1 Corinthians 12:3b:

Who is Jesus to <u>you</u>?

11. Why do you think Jesus told them not to reveal His identity?

12. In what must have seemed a disappointment to the disciples, which prophecy did Jesus give them? (v.31)

    Describe the reaction of Peter in Matthew 16:22.

13. Why was Peter so crushed at this revelation?

    What kind of Messiah were the people expecting?

    Answer using the following:

    Genesis 49:10:

1 Samuel 2:10:

Psalm 21:5:

Isaiah 49:5-6:

Jeremiah 23:5-6:

Zechariah 9:9:

14. In verse 33. who did Jesus say was behind Peter's spiritual blindness in regard to the Divine plan?

   Discuss this further using the following scriptures:

   Romans 8:5:

   1 Corinthians 2:14:

   2 Corinthians 4:4:

15. What is required of any who would follow Christ? (v.34-35)

   What does this mean in your life?

16. Read verses 36-37. What did the apostle Paul say about losing his life for Christ?

   Acts 20:23-24:

Acts 21:13:

Philippians 1:20:

Philippians 3:7-14:

17. What is Jesus' warning in verse 38? (Also see Matthew 10:33)

Let us be able to say in accordance with Romans 1:16:
"I am not ashamed of the gospel of Christ: for it is the power of God unto salvation to everyone that believeth.

Lesson Twelve: Mark 9:1-29

"... He was transfigured before them."
- Mark 9:2

"And there was a cloud that overshadowed them: and a voice came out of the cloud, saying, 'This is my beloved Son: hear Him.'"
- Mark 9:7

"And the Word was made flesh, and dwelt among us, (and we beheld His glory, the glory as of the only begotten of the Father), full of grace and truth."
- John 1: 14

"For we have not followed cunningly devised fables, when we made known unto you the power and coming of our Lord Jesus Christ, but were eyewitnesses of His majesty. For He received from God the Father honor and glory, when there came such a voice to Him from the excellent glory, 'This is my beloved Son, in whom I am well pleased.' And this voice which came from heaven we heard, when we were with Him in the holy mount."
- 2 Peter 1: 16-18

Peter, James, and John were tremendously honored to see the transfiguration of Jesus Christ up on the mount, witnessing Him in His glory, shining as bright as the sun. Yet, as they were overcome by this glorious, heavenly sight, and desiring their experience to last forever, the conversation between Jesus and His two companions had a definite earthly theme. Moses, the giver of the Law (which in every detail typifies the Messiah) stood with Jesus, as well as Elijah, the most honored of the prophets, the man who did not see death, but was taken up to be with the Lord. Elijah also had the honor of being a type of John the Baptist, the forerunner of the Messiah.

What was the subject of their discourse? Luke tells us, "His decease which He should accomplish at Jerusalem."[24] Notice that Jesus' death would be something which He accomplished - as he said in John 10:18, "No man taketh it [my life] from me, but I lay it down of myself. I have the power to lay it down, and power to take it again." Even though Jesus had begun to speak

---
[24] Luke 9:31

of His coming death to His disciples, they did not want to believe it, thinking as we do at the reception of bad news, "It must be some horrible mistake!" However, Moses and Elijah both knew that the long foretold death and resurrection of Jesus Christ was the only means of salvation for a lost race, and looked forward to the new dispensation, which would see the fulfillment of both "the law and the prophets."[25] As 2 Corinthians 3:11 puts it, "If that which is done away [the law] was glorious, much more that which remains is glorious."

The New Covenant, accomplished by Jesus' death and resurrection, has given Christians our whole reason for living, our entire hope in this world and the next. Praise God that Jesus did not stay on the mount in heavenly glory - but that He went down to His death to make the kingdom of heaven accessible to men!

Read Mark 9:1-29

Please **pray** for the guidance of the Holy Spirit before answering the questions.

1. What did Jesus promise to some of His disciples?
   (v.1)

2. What is the kingdom of God?
   Answer using these scriptures.

   Matthew 12:28:

   Luke 10:9:

   Luke 17: 20, 21:

---

[25] Matthew 5:17-18

3. Is this (v. 1) a possibility for any of us in this dispensation?
   Answer using the following scriptures:

   1 Thessalonians 4:16-17:

   Matthew 24:29-31:

   Matthew 25:31-34:

   Jude 14:

   Revelation 19:11-16

4. What took place six days later? (v.2-3)
   (For more detail read Luke 9:28-29; Matthew 17:1-2)

5. Has anyone seen the glory of the Father?
   (See Exodus 33:20)

   How then, can we see the Father?
   Use the following to answer:

   Hebrews 1:3a:

   John 1: 14:

   John 14:7-9:

   In light of 1 John 3:2, describe the hope that you live for as a Christian.
   (Also see Colossians 3:4)

6. Read v.4, as well as Luke 9:30,31.
   Whom did Jesus talk with, and what did they discuss?

   What is Moses known for? (John 1:17a)

   What is Elijah known for 2 Kings 2:1,11; 1 Kings 18:36-39

   Why would the death of Jesus be important to these glorified saints?
   (Refer to Genesis 3:15, 12:3, 17:5-7; Hebrews 11:24- 27;
   1 Peter 1: 10-11; Job 19:25; Psalm 40:7)

7. Why is Jesus' death important to you?

   Share a favorite scripture concerning your salvation.

8. What was Peter's foolish remark in v.5-6?

   Why did he say it?

   Write these proverbs on the tongue:

   Proverbs 17:27-28:

   Proverbs 13:3:

9. What was God's admonition to the disciples? (v.7; Hebrews 1:1-2)

   Why? (Ecclesiastes 5:2)

   How is your prayer time with the Lord? Who does most of the talking?

10. What should you be prepared to say at all times? (1 Samuel 3:10)

11. When Jesus was left alone with the disciples, what did He command them? (v.9)
    Did they do this? (2 Peter 1:16-18; John 1:1-2)

12. What were the disciples puzzled about? (v.10)

    Using 1 Corinthians 15, discuss the resurrection of the believer.

13. Read Malachi 4:5-6.

    Who is Jesus referring to, who was His forerunner?
    (See Luke 1:13-17; Matthew 11:13-14)

14. How does the parable of the vineyard describe both the fate of John and of Jesus? (See Luke 20:9-16)

15. What was the scene Jesus encountered at the foot of the mountain? (v.14-18)

    How did He rebuke the scribes? (v.16)

16. Consider verse 19. What does this show you about the Lord? (Also see Genesis 6:3a)

    God is gracious! Yet, what does Paul say in Galatians 2:21 and Ephesians 4:30?

    Think carefully: Who was included in the "faithless generation"?

Are you failing to be effective for God because of your lack of faith?

17. What was the condition of the child? (v.20-22)

    As the man pleaded for help, what was Jesus' reply? (v.23)

    Describe the humble confession of the father (v.24).

18. Describe in your own words, the three kinds of unbelief shown in this chapter, considering the scribes, the disciples, and the father of the boy.

19. Recount the casting out of the foul spirit (v.25-27)

How did Jesus say this kind of spirit was cast out? (v.29)
Is the Lord calling you to fast and pray for a person or situation?
If so, be obedient!
Keep in mind, however, Psalm 51:16,17:
"For thou desirest not sacrifice; else I would give it: thou delightest not in burnt offering. The sacrifices of God are a broken spirit: a broken and a contrite heart, O God, thou wilt not despise."

Lesson Thirteen: Mark 9:30-50

> "If any man desire to be first, the same shall be the last of all, and the servant of all."
>
> - Mark 9:35

> "Only with pride comes contention."
>
> - Proverbs 13:10

> "Let nothing be done through strife or vainglory; but in lowliness of mind let each esteem the other better than themselves."
>
> - Philippians 2:3

As Jesus continued His inexorable progress toward the cross, He continued to tell the disciples more and more plainly that His earthly life was corning to an end, but they would not receive this from Him. Perhaps they could not. They were not yet ready to join the fellowship of His sufferings.

Instead we find these men puffed up with pride, the very sin that caused Lucifer to be cast down from heaven. The pride of life, as 1John 2:16 tells us, is not of the Father, but of the world. And who is the prince of this world? Satan, the father of pride! Jesus made it clear very quickly that greatness is to be found in servitude, even servitude to those you consider your equals of inferiors - even the Son of Man came not to be ministered unto, but to minister, and to give His life a ransom for many. Oswald Chambers, in one of his devotional books, asks some very piercing questions of the Christian minister: "Are you ready to be offered up? ... Are you ready to be not so much as a drop in the bucket - to be so hopelessly insignificant that you are never thought of again in connection with the life you served? Are you willing to spend and be spent, not seeking to be ministered unto, but to minister?"[26] Sadly, like the disciples, most Christians today must confess that the answer is "No". We want to be noticed and commended - how much work our Lord has to do in us to bring us to a point of maturity, humility, Christlikeness, so that others might see Christ in us, not us!

Jesus tells us in this chapter also, to make no sectarian distinctions, but to seek fellowship with true believers of every kind. God does miracles in many and diverse settings - do not box Him in to *your* church!

---

[26] Oswald Chambers, *My Utmost For His Highest* (Dodd, Mead &Co. Inc., 1935).

Our chapter closes with Jesus' command that we have salt in ourselves, that salt of preparation for the sacrifice of fire. One day, each believer's work shall be tried by fire[27]- that it may be found to be pure. The work to be tested begins today as we give ourselves in humility to Christ as "a living sacrifice, holy, acceptable unto God."[28] Only then will prideful contentions cease, when we have given ourselves to God as His lowliest of His servants!

---

[27] 1 Corinthians 3:13
[28] Romans 12:1

Dana Kruckenberg Thompson

Read Mark 9:30-50

Please **pray** for the guidance of the Holy Spirit before answering the questions.

1. What was now to become the theme of Jesus' teaching the disciples? (v.31)

    Why? Answer using the following:

    Genesis 3:15:

    Psalm 22:1,13-18:

    Isaiah 53:10-11:

    Luke 24:44-46:

    John 3:17:

    John 6:51:

2. Describe the disciples' reaction in v.32.

    Use these scriptures to explain their spiritual condition.

    Mark 8:17-21:

    Matthew 16:21-23:

3. What did it take for the disciples to understand His saying? (See John 2:19-22)

4. The disciples argued along the way to Capernaum. What were they arguing about?

   Did they admit it?

   How did Jesus know anyway? Answer based on the following:

   Luke 9:46-47:

   Mark 2:6-8:

   1 Kings 8:39:

   Psalm 94:9-11:

   Amos 4:13:

5. Has the Lord convicted you of comparing yourself or your ministry with someone else?
   Share if you would, what the Lord shown you.

   What does 1 Corinthians 13:4 say? (See also 2 Corinthians 10:12)

6. Tell what Jesus' statement in v.35 could mean in *your* life. (Refer to James 4:6)

7. What blessing is promised to anyone who receives a child in the name of Jesus? (v.37)

   Describe how Matthew 25:34-40 further expounds upon this concept.

8. Regrettably, what had the disciples done to another believer? (v.38)

   Had this person's ministry met with success?

   Compare with Mark 9:17-18. What, perhaps could have been the disciples' motive? Give your opinion.

Confess to the Lord right now any feelings of envy and competitiveness in regard to another's ministry for Christ!

9. Consider verses 39-40 carefully. How did Jesus view this individual? Also refer to 1 Corinthians 12:3.

10. Does God take notice of and regard even a small kindness done in His name?

    Summarize the following to help you answer:

    Luke 6:35:

    Romans 2:10:

    1 Corinthians 3:8:

    Psalm 41:1:

Isaiah 58:10-11:

Zechariah 7:9-10:

Matthew 5:7:

Ephesians 6:8:

James 1:27:

1 John 3:17-18:

Acts 20:35:

Hebrews 6:10:

11. What warning does Jesus give in verse 42?

    Who are the "little ones"?

    Consult these verses:

    Matthew 5:45:

    Mark 10:24:

    Luke 20:36:

    John 13:33:

12. How does Jesus, in v.43-47, compare the saving of your physical body to the saving of your soul?

13. What did Paul say about the "members", or parts, or our bodies? Answer using the following:

    Romans 7:18:

    Romans 6:13,19:

14. How is Hell described by Jesus?

*Do you have loved ones headed for this fate in eternity?
Please make a commitment to pray for them diligently and to witness to them regularly!*

15. How were sacrifices prepared according to the Law of Moses? (See Leviticus 2:13)

16. Can we be a sacrifice for Christ? (See Philippians 2:17)

    Literally:
    2 Timothy 4:6:

    Figuratively:
    Romans 12:1:

17. How can we be salt? Answer using the following:

Matthew 5:13,16:

Colossians 4:6:

18. What is a Christian's goal in relationship to others? (v.50)

Summarize the following:

Romans 14:19:

2 Corinthians 13:11:

Hebrews 12:14:

Commit James 3:18 to heart:
"The fruit of righteousness is sown in peace of them that make peace."

Lesson Fourteen: Mark 10:1-27

> "From the beginning of the creation God made them male and female. For this cause shall a man leave his father and mother, and cleave to his wife: And the two shall become one flesh; so then they are no longer two, but one flesh. Therefore what God has joined together, let not man put asunder."
> - Mark 10:6-9

> "The Lord God of Israel says, that He hates divorce ..."
> - Malachi 2:16

At the time the Pharisees came to Jesus with their question about divorce, there was a strong public controversy taking place between two schools of Jewish thought. The school of Hillel stated that a man might divorce his wife for any cause; the school of Shammai opined that divorce was unlawful except in cases of adultery. The design of the Pharisees was to embroil Jesus in this controversy, and to alienate Him from one or the other of the parties.

Rather than walk into their trap, Jesus first turned their attention to the law of Moses. The Pharisees had referred to Deuteronomy 24:1,2:

> "When a man has taken a wife, and married her, and it come to pass that she find no favor in his eyes because he has found some uncleanness in her: then let him write her a bill of divorcement, and give it in her hand, and send her out of his house. And when she is departed out of his house, she may go and be another man's wife."

Moses had only permitted divorce because of hardened, stiff-necked, cruel men, who were already in the habit of divorcing their wives at will. Moses' law was at least an attempt to regulate and formalize the proceeding, to cause a man to seek consultation, and perhaps reconsider his actions.

In God's eyes, however, this was not satisfactory, for there is a higher law than Moses': the law of God. The law of God not only expresses His holy character, but His perfect will for man, and to this Jesus refers in verses 6-9 of our chapter. On the occasion of the very first marriage in Genesis 3, God spoke, once and for all time - that a man shall be joined to his wife, and the two shall become one flesh - no longer two, but one person. This bond must not be broken but by the One who created it, at His appointed time, at the hour of the death of one of the spouses.

God hates divorce! Yet God knew that human beings are fallen creatures living in a fallen world, and that sin would enter in to the marriage bond to destroy it, in the form of adultery. Therefore in Matthew 19: 9, Jesus gave the only scriptural grounds for divorce. "And I say to you, whoever divorces his wife, except for sexual immorality, and marries another, commits adultery." And His Word stands across the centuries, despite any man-made disclaimers of "mitigating circumstances," "incompatibility" or "a different society." Why? Because God says in Malachi 3:6, "I am the LORD, I change not."

A Christian in a marital crisis today must ask him or herself one question: Will I stand with my God and His word in my hour of trial, with a clear conscience, or will I commit a sin against Him which I will regret for the rest of my life? Only you and the Lord know how you will answer that question.

Read Mark 10:1-27
Please **pray** for the guidance of the Holy Spirit before you answer the questions.

1. What did Jesus continue to do as he entered Judea? (v.1)

    How was this prophesied?
    (See Deuteronomy 18:15-19; John 4:25; Acts 3:19-26)

2. Was Judea a safe place for Jesus to go?
    (Refer to the following to answer: John 7:1-13; 8:56-59; 11:7-8; Luke 9:51)

3. Whom would He be certain to encounter? (v.2)
    What was their attitude toward Jesus?
    (Refer to John 9:16-22; Mark 12:13; Luke 11:53-54)

4. In light of their attitude, what controversy were the Pharisees attempting to entangle Jesus in? (v.2)

   Discuss the wisdom of Jesus' answer in v~3.

   Give other examples of His method of answering the Pharisees (and others)
   from any of the gospels.

5. What did Moses' law say regarding this topic? (Summarize Deuteronomy 24:1-2)

   How did the Pharisees subtly distort Moses' regulation?
   (See Matthew 19:7)

6. Why did Moses even have to allow divorce at all? (v.5)

   Look up the reasons within these verses as well:

   Exodus 32:9:

   2 Kings 17:13-14:

   Nehemiah 9:13-16:

7. Even higher than Moses' law, what does the Law of God say about marriage?
   Summarize verses 6-9 in your own words.

   If you are married, what does this mean to you?

8. Why were even the offerings of the Jews being cursed?
   Read and summarize Malachi 2:13-16

9. Is any law of man's regarding marriage, now or in the future, able to supersede God's law, in His eyes?

   Why? (v.9; Acts 5:29)

Pray about this question:
Are you willing to suffer any kind of unhappiness rather than disobey God?

   Summarize and meditate on the following verses:

   Luke 6:46:

   John 14:15,21:

   1 John 2:3-5:

   Acts 24:16:

10. How did Jesus continue to clarify His word about divorce to the disciples? (v.11-12)

    What are the only grounds for divorce?

   Give to the Lord today your personal commitment to your marriage!

11. Who came to Jesus in v.13

   What was the disciple's reaction?

   Give your opinion: What might have been his reason? (Mark 1:37)

12. How did Jesus receive the children? (v.14)

   Can the attitude of children show us the kingdom of God? (v. 15)

   See and write Matthew 18:4:

13. How was Jesus' action in verse 16 prophesied?
   See and write Isaiah 40:11:

   Write these scriptures which remind us to have Jesus' attitude toward children.

   Psalm 127:3-5:

   Psalm 113:9:

   Psalm 107:41:

14. Read Luke 18:18-23

   Who came running to Jesus?

   How did he address Jesus? (Mark 10:17)

   What did Jesus call his attention to? (v.18)

Write these scriptures on the goodness of God:

   Psalm 36:7:

   Psalm 107:8-9:

   Isaiah 63:7:

15. Did Jesus actually refuse worship?
    Cite these instances to form your opinion:

    Matthew 8:2-3:

    Matthew 14:29-33:

    John 9:37-38:

    John 12:3:

16. What was the young ruler's character? (v.19-20)

    Can anyone really obey all of the law?
    (See Acts 15:7-10, James 2:10, Romans 3:23)

17. Can obeying the law save you?
    (See Ephesians 2:8-9)

18. What did this man lack? (v.21)

Therefore, what was his sin? (v.22)

(Also see Exodus 20:17; Job 20:15; Luke 12:15)

19. What statements did Jesus make in regard to those who trust in riches? (v.23-25)

    Consider these scriptures:

    Job 31:24,25,28

    Proverbs 15:27

    Proverbs 23:4-5

    Proverbs 30:8-9

    1 Timothy 6:17

20. What can happen to the covetous Christian?
    (Refer to 1 Timothy 6:9-10)

Search your heart! Is covetousness overtaking you, replacing your desire for the things of God? If so, make confession right now!

21. Who only can save (or condemn) both rich and poor? (v.27)
    (Also see Revelation 20:11-12)

*Remember Acts 10:34 "God is no respecter of persons."
And may his attitude be ours!*

Lesson Fifteen: Mark 10:28-52

> "What things were gain to me, these I have counted loss for Christ. But indeed I also count all things loss for the excellence of the knowledge of Christ Jesus my Lord, for whom I have suffered the loss of all things, and count them as rubbish, that I may gain Christ ... that I may know Him and the power of His resurrection, and the fellowship of His sufferings ..."
> - Philippians 3:7,8,10

> "Whosoever will be great among you, shall be your minister: And whosoever of you will be chiefest, shall be servant of all. For even the Son of Man came not to be ministered unto, but to minister, and to give His life a ransom for many."
> - Mark 10:43-45

In the second part of Mark chapter 10, we see Jesus' own definition of greatness - not greatness as we know it, but greatness in the kingdom of God. There is not a sincere Christian who has not asked at one time or another, "What does the Lord require of me, that I might become a true disciple of His, and be used to bring glory to His Name, and to further the cause of the kingdom of God on the earth?" Our Savior points out three characteristics, (indeed, requirements) of those who would serve Christ:

1. Abandon all to Christ. Peter states in verse 28, "Lo, we all, and have followed thee." Must a Christian leave family, and property literally in order to follow Christ? Many have, serving the Lord Jesus in unheard-of, far-flung reaches of the earth. God may call you to such a ministry one day, for He said Himself, that "the harvest truly is great, but the laborers are few."[29]
For most Christians, however, abandonment to Christ has a more figurative, spiritual, but no less compelling meaning. And no less difficult, because of the subtle nature of the changes which must take place in the mind and heart. To be abandoned to Christ is to be able to say, "to live is Christ, to die is gain,"[30] Whether the Lord should confine me to my home entirely, send me thousands of miles away, or allow any condition in between, makes no difference. Whether I will be single all my life, or raise a family makes no difference; it is Jesus I live for, not the people or circumstances He allows in

---
[29] Luke 10:2
[30] Philippians 1:21

my life. Can I truly say with Job, "Though He slay me, yet will I trust in Him"?[31] Abandon all to Christ - and watch everything else pale in comparison!

2. Become a servant - humble yourself as Christ did. Do most of us have any concept today of what it means to be a servant? From the wealthiest to the least prosperous, we Christians today spend our lives with others waiting on us, doing our bidding, in public and in the home. Look at Jesus Christ, the Lord of glory, who "made Himself of no reputation, and took upon Him the form of a servant, and was made in the likeness of men: and being found in fashion as a man, He humbled Himself, and became obedient unto death, even the death of the cross."[32] Yet many of us will not so much as do childcare so that someone else might benefit from a Bible study, or clean up dishes and dump wastebaskets after a potluck, particularly if it is unlikely that anyone of note will find out about it. We have no desire or intention of serving obscure people in obscure places: like James and John, we want the most prominent places of "service". Whom do we desire to serve? Jesus? If so, remember that He said, "Whatever you have done to the least of these, my brethren, you have done unto me."[33] Or do we desire to serve ourselves and our reputations, always garnering praises and more and more visibility at church? Praise God that He is the One who rewards and recognizes the true servant, according to His righteous and holy standards! God also knows our motives - and all the "ministry" in the world cannot hide a self-seeking heart.

3. Be ready, prepared, and willing to partake of Jesus' cup and Jesus' baptism ~ to join the fellowship of His suffering. This facet of following Christ is most frightening to us, because we are not told ahead of time which form of suffering the Lord will allow in each of our lives. We are told, however, in John 16:33, "In the world you shall have tribulation," and in verse 30 of our chapter, that we will receive "persecutions." Many Christians, from the earliest days of the church to this day, have been physically persecuted, hounded from city to city, and even martyred for their faith. Others have faced complete rejection and ostracism from family, friends, and associates. Often, devoted saints find themselves growing weary striving against sin, or discouraged that others will not make Jesus Lord of their lives. Some suffer the painful degeneration of their bodies or equally painful degeneration of their families. Yet, Jesus' words reassure us most in the dark hours, that He is merciful, gracious, ever-present, and that He has overcome the world. For

---

[31] Job 13:15
[32] Philippians 2:7-8
[33] Matthew 25:40

every loss we suffer, we shall receive one hundred times as many blessings in our lifetime here on earth, and as if that were not enough! - eternal life with Him in the world to come.

Jesus came to give His life a ransom for many, offering salvation to all mankind as a gift. But the rewards for one who would identify with Christ are earned, and that identification comes hard in the days of our flesh! Therefore we must apply daily to the Lord for a refilling of His Spirit. For there is no testing which He will allow without giving us all of Himself that we need to accomplish His work in us.

If it is your desire to be all that God wants you to be, go to Jesus, whose ears are ever open to His children's prayers!

Read Mark 10:28-52

Please **pray** before answering the questions.

1. After seeing how the rich young man refused to give up his possessions to follow Christ, what did Peter remark? (v.28)

2. Write these verses on following Christ:

   Matthew 4:18-20:

   Matthew 16:24:

   John 12:26:

   Luke 9:62:

Have you truly set aside all distractions, "gotten up", and followed Christ?

Have you "put your hand to the plow"?

3. Re-read v.29-30. How does Jesus rate following and furthering the gospel in comparison with relationships with other people, and other temporal concerns? (v.29) (Also see Matthew 10:37; Luke 14:26)

4. What is the reward for being willing to let all other relationships and concerns go, in order to put Christ first? (v.30)

   Have you seen this come true in your life?

5. What else can the disciple of Jesus expect in addition to rewards? (v.30) Summarize these verses:

   Matthew 10:16:

   Matthew 24:9:

   Mark 13:9:

   Luke 21:12-17:

   John 15:18-19:

6. Are we to live in fear as followers of Christ? Why not?
   (See Matthew 10:28; Mark 9:42; Luke 21:18-19; 2 Corinthians 6:4-10)

7. What is our ultimate reward? (v.30)

   What is it according to these verses?

Mark 8:35:

Hebrews 11:13-16:

Luke 6:22-23:

2 Corinthians 4:16-18:

8. In verse 32, we read that the disciples were amazed and afraid on the way to Jerusalem.
   Why? (Also refer to John 11:7-8)

   What did Jesus reveal to them in v.33-34?

   How does verse 33 show that all of mankind was represented in the killing of Jesus? (See Acts 4:25-27)

   Why was this necessary? Write the answers found in the following passages:

   Romans 3:9-10:

   Romans 3:19 (last phrase):

   1 John 2:2:

   How did the crucifixion become a blessing to all mankind, even as prophesied?

   Summarize these verses:

Psalm 86:9:

Isaiah 11:10:

Isaiah 40:5:

Daniel 7:13-14:

John 10:16:

Romans 3:29:

9. How did James and John approach Jesus in v.35?

    Might this have been justified? (See John 14:13-14; 15:7)

    What was their actual request in verse 37?

    How did this show an abuse of their privilege to petition the Lord? (Refer to James 4:3)

    What is the conditional promise given to *all* believers in 1 John 5:14-15?

10. Despite their impropriety and imprudence, what does v.37 show that these men believed about Jesus?

    Additionally, write these scriptures:

Isaiah 9:6-7:

Zechariah 9:9-10:

Matthew 25:31-34:

1 Timothy 6:15:

Daniel 7:13,18:

11. What does Jesus ask them in v. 38?

    Discuss "the baptism" and "the cup", using these scriptures:

    Luke 12:49:50:

    Romans 6:3-4:

    Luke 22:20:

    Matthew 26:37-44:

    John 18:11:

12. Give your opinion: What does James and John's quick reply in v.39 show about them? (Also see Mark 8:21)

13. What did eventually happen to James and John?

Acts 12:1-2:

Revelation 1:9:

14. Why was it not Jesus' decision to give the places on His right hand and on His left? (v.40)

   For whom are places prepared? (See Matthew 8:11; 25:21,34; John 12:26; John 14:1-3; Revelation 3:21)

15. Why were the ten other disciples so displeased with James and John?

   What did Jesus need to remind them all of once again in v.42-44? (Also see Mark 9:35)

16. In which role did Jesus come? (v.45)

   What does this mean to you in your walk today?
   Will you lay down your life, take up your cross daily, and
   follow Jesus as a servant, and a living sacrifice?

17. Despite discouragement from the people, what did blind Bartimaeus do as Jesus approached? (v.47,48)

   Share the spiritual principle found here, using these verses:

   Psalm 55:16-17:

   Luke 11:5-10:

18. Did Jesus receive Bartimaeus?

   Will He receive you and your petition?

   Psalm 10:17:

   Psalm 91:15:

19. How was Bartimaeus commended by our Lord? (v.52)

   And how was he rewarded?

   Thank you, Lord, that your ears are always open to our prayers, to them who call upon you with a pure heart!

Lesson Sixteen: Mark 11

"Know therefore, and understand that from the going forth of the commandment to restore and to build Jerusalem unto the Messiah the Prince shall be seven weeks, and threescore and two weeks..."
- Daniel 9:25

"Rejoice greatly, O daughter of Zion! Shout, O daughter of Jerusalem!
Behold, your King is coming to you; He is just and having salvation, lowly and riding on a donkey, a colt, the foal of a donkey."
- Zechariah 9:9

"'Behold, I send my messenger and He will prepare the way before me. And the Lord, whom you seek will suddenly come to His temple, even the Messenger of the Covenant, in whom you delight. Behold, He is coming.' Thus says the Lord of hosts...

'He will sit as a refiner and a purifier of silver; He will purify the sons of Levi, and purge them as gold and silver, that they may offer to the Lord an offering in righteousness.'"
- Malachi 3:1,3

Jesus Christ's coming into Jerusalem, which we refer to as the "Triumphal Entry," was spoken of by the prophets hundreds of years before it took place. Daniel 9 tells us that from the decree by King Artaxerxes to allow the Jews to rebuild the temple[34] to Messiah's entry into Jerusalem would be four hundred eighty-three years, or 173,880 days. Jesus' procession took place on March 29, A.D. 33, the exact day!

The very words the crowd shouted, "Blessed is He that comes in the Name of the Lord: we have blessed you out of the house of the Lord" are in Psalm 118. Zechariah 9:9 foretold the manner of Jesus' coming, on the foal of a donkey, emblematic of royalty. Mules and donkeys were the mounts chosen by kings when they came in peace; the horse was used for war. Solomon at his inauguration rode on King David's mule.[35] So Jesus' entry was not one of poverty or degradation but of the dignity befitting the Prince of Peace.

---
[34] Nehemiah 2:1-8
[35] 1 Kings 1:33

The triumphal entry actually took place on three separate days, with our Lord spending the nights in between in Bethany, outside Jerusalem. Our passage in Malachi deals with one of the events of the second day the cleansing of the temple. The Feast of Passover was approaching and all Jewish males were required to go to Jerusalem to the temple to offer sacrifice. Because the required doves would be difficult to transport from a distance, vendors sold them in the outer court. There was also traffic in oil, incense, and wine. Roman coins were the currency of the civilized world at that time, so moneychangers sat at the temple to provide the required temple offering of half a shekel.[36] The goods were sold at inflated prices (much the same as modern tourist attractions!) and the moneychangers demanded a small sum for each exchange. Our Lord did not exaggerate when He called the temple "a den of thieves" -so it was. The fact that the people obeyed the Lord after He overturned the tables (in that they carried no more wares into the temple) shows that they recognized His authority - the authority of the Messiah, the Savior of Israel.

But we know Jesus as the Savior of the whole world. And when He comes into a life, He also "cleanses the temple," that we might become a fit dwelling place for His Holy Spirit.
2 Corinthians 6:16 tells us that we are "the temple of the living God." As we know, a holy God will not coexist with sin; therefore, our temples must be free of defilement caused by worldly lusts and the resulting sins we so easily fall prey to. How wonderful to know from 1 John 1:9, that the blood of Christ continues to cleanse us as often as we confess and repent of our sins!

How blessed it is to know that the blood of Christ is ever available and efficacious to those who call upon Him!

Lord, grant that we might be open and honest with you concerning our sin, that our "temples" might be honorable and pleasing dwelling places for your Spirit!

---

[36] Exodus 30:13-15

Dana Kruckenberg Thompson

Read Mark 11

Please **pray** for the guidance of the Holy Spirit as you answer the questions.

1. What was the errand Jesus sent two of the disciples on? (v.2-3)

   What could be the significance of the face that the colt had never been ridden?

   Read and consider:

   Isaiah 7:14:

   Luke 23:50-53:

2. What were they to tell anyone who questioned their actions? (v.3)

   Why did the owners allow the colt to go? (v.6)

   Did they know Jesus, there in Bethany? (See John 12:1,2, 9-11)

3. What kind of colt did He ride? (Consider Zechariah 9:9)

   How do Old Testament scriptures confirm New Testament scriptures? Answer using the following:

   1 Peter 1:10-11:

   2 Peter 1: 20-21:

4. Describe Jesus' procession into Jerusalem. (v.7-10)

Compare with Luke 19:37-38
At which other event was the same praise (in Luke19:38) given? (See Luke 2:12-14)

5. What is the significance of "the kingdom of our father David" in verse 10?

   Answer by summarizing the following:

   2 Samuel 7:11-16:

   Psalm 89:19-20;27-29;34-37:

   Isaiah 9:6-7:

   Isaiah 22:22:

   Revelation 3:7:

   Revelation 22:16:

6. Read Matthew 21:15 and describe the chief priests' and scribes' objection to the praises given to Jesus.

   What was Jesus' reply? (Matthew 21:16)

   Are your little ones following your example and singing praises to God?

7. Describe the incident of the fig tree in verses 13-14;20-21.

Consider the spiritual significance:

Psalm 1:1-3:

Luke 13:6-9:

John 15:1-6:

*Are you bearing fruit for God?
Or have you allowed yourself to be barren and unfruitful?*

8. Describe Jesus' actions in the temple (v.15-16) and compare with John 2:14-16.

   Why was Jesus angered? (v.17)

   Write the scriptures He was quoting:

   Isaiah 56:7:

   Jeremiah 7:11:

9. Which words of Old Testament scripture did the Holy Spirit quicken to John's mind (See John 2:17) as he recalled Jesus' cleansing of the temple? (Hint: Psalm 69:9)

10. What can we learn from Jesus' anger?

    Psalm 7:11b:

Ephesians 4:6a:

Ask yourself: "Is my anger righteous, and directed against sin, or is it the result of pride - spiteful, cruel, and vengeful?" Ask God to deal with any unrighteous anger in your life!

11. Why did the scribes and chief priests seek a way to destroy Jesus? (v.18; John 12:19; John 11:45-57; Matthew 27:18)

12. What did the people think of Jesus? (v.18; Luke 19:47-48; John 12:42)

13. After Peter's comment on the withered fig tree, how did Jesus use this opportunity to strengthen their faith? (v.22-24)

    Write these scriptures of praying in faith:

    Matthew 7:7:

    John 14:13:

    John 15:7:

    John 16:24:

    James 1:5-6:

    James 5:15:

Are your prayers getting answered? Why or why not?

14. What does Jesus remind us to do before we pray? (v.25; Matthew 5:23-24)

    Why must we forgive others? (v.26)

15. What is the main point of the story in Matthew 18:23-35?

    Keep in mind that harboring unforgiveness in your heart will render your prayer life useless!

16. How did the chief priests, scribes, and elders confront Jesus? (v.27-28)

    Again, what method did Jesus use with these men? (v.30)

    Describe their puzzlement. (v.31-32)

17. Consider carefully: If these hypocrites acknowledged John, whom also must they acknowledge?

    Why? Answer based on the following:

    Luke 1:13-17:

    Luke 3:2-4;15-16:

    John 1:21-34:

    What was the outright lie the men told in verse 33?

Was Jesus under any obligation at all to answer them? (v.33)
Why? (See Job 33:13)

Dear Lord, we thank you for who You are! And when we get tempted to question your doings, help us to remember that your work is "honorable and glorious: and your righteousness endures forever."

Lesson Seventeen: Mark 12

"You are a holy people to the Lord your God; the Lord your God has chosen you to be a people for Himself, a special treasure above all the peoples on the face of the earth."
- Deuteronomy 7:6

"... Israelites, to whom pertain the adoption, the glory, the covenants, the giving of the law, the service of God, and the promises; Of whom are the fathers and from whom, according to the flesh, Christ came, who is over all, the eternally blessed God."
- Romans 9:4-5

"He will be as a sanctuary, but a stone of stumbling and a rock of offense to both houses of Israel, as a trap and a snare to the inhabitants of Jerusalem. And many among them shall stumble; they shall fall and be broken, be snared and taken."
Isaiah 8:14

"O Jerusalem, Jerusalem, the one who kills the prophets and stones those who are sent to her! How often I wanted to gather your children together, as a hen gathers her chicks under her wings, but you were not willing! Behold, your house is left to you desolate."
- Matthew 23:37-38

God chose Israel to be His people, His peculiar treasure. As Romans 9:4-5 tells us, He had vouchsafed to them exclusively the knowledge of Himself, and given them the only religion He has ever given to any nation. He gave them the law, the promises, the service of the tabernacle, even His own shekinah glory! Most glorious of all, God chose the Jewish race to provide the human side of His only Son, Jesus Christ the Messiah. No nation has ever been given the privileges of relationship with God that He gave to the Jews!

Yet their history, as recorded both in the law and the prophets, is one of continual rebellion against the God who loved them so much. As far back as Deuteronomy 6:15, God warned them through Moses that if they turned away from Him, He would destroy them from the face of the earth. (For a complete history of the curses which have come upon the nation Israel, see

Deuteronomy 28:15-68).

Throughout the centuries, God sent His prophets, one after another, to warn His people to turn from their wickedness and obey Him, that they might be blessed and restored, rather than cursed and scattered. Lastly, God sent His own son, Jesus, bringing salvation to all who would believe, to the Jew first, and then and only then, to the Gentiles.

The parable of the vineyard in our chapter brings forth the history of the nation. The vineyard represents Israel: entrusted with the things of God, the servants, and the prophets. The prophets came one by one with their messages and were met with beating, stoning, torture, and death.[37] Jesus was also put to death by the religious rulers who wanted to keep their "place and nation,"[38] rather than submit themselves to God, accept their Messiah and be saved. But it was God's will to sacrifice His Son, and their hostility was only an instrument in God's plan to bless all of mankind. Once again, God made the wrath of man to praise Him![39]

By passing judgment upon the wicked husbandmen of the parable, the scribes, elders, and chief priests described their own fate, for God indeed allowed Jerusalem to be completely destroyed in 70 A.D. by the Roman general Titus. As Jesus had prophesied in Matthew 24:2, not one stone was left upon another.

Jesus is the chief cornerstone; the founder, author, and finisher of our faith. Will you build your life on this foundation, or will it fall upon you, as it did the Jews, and grind you to powder?

Read Mark 12

Please **pray** before answering the questions.

1. Read the parable of the vineyard, v.1-8.
   Whom do the servants represent?

---

[37] Hebrews 11:35-38
[38] John 11:47-53
[39] Psalm 76:10

Can you name some of these men from scripture who were thus shamefully treated?

    Give chapter and verse. For reference, see Hebrews 11:35-38.

2. Who are the wicked husbandmen?

    How did Jesus describe their actions in past history?

    Consider the following:

    Romans 10:21:

    Matthew 23:29-36:

    Numbers 14:18:

3. Israel has often been pictured in scripture as a vineyard.

    Write these verses:

    Psalm 80:8:

    Song of Solomon 8:11-12:

    Jeremiah 2:21:

    Read Isaiah 5:1-7 carefully. How might this describe the fate of the nation?

4. Describe the son in the parable using verse 6.

    Write the following verses:

    John 1:18:

    Mark 1:11:

    Luke 9:35:

    What did the owner hope the husbandmen would do? (v.6)

    But what happened?

    Write the following verses:

    John 1:11:

    Isaiah 53:3:

    John 12:37:

5. Why did the husbandmen kill their heir?

    What did the Jewish rulers hope to accomplish by killing Jesus? (See John 11:46-53; 12:9-11,19)

    How did Caiaphas prophesy? (v.49-52)

6. Read v. 9, and compare with Matthew 21:40-41.

    How did the men pronounce their own fate, and that of the Jewish nation?

    Refer to the following verses:

    Isaiah 11:10:

    Hosea 2:23:

    Matthew 12:18-21:

    John 10:16:

    Matthew 8:10-12:

    Acts 13:44-48:

7. Discuss "the stone which the builders rejected" using these scriptures:

    Psalm 118:22-23:

    Romans 9:31-33; 10:1-3:

    Discuss Christ as the cornerstone of the church:

    Acts 4:10-12:

    1 Corinthians 3:9-11:

Ephesians 2:19-22:

1 Peter 2:4-8:

8. What else did Jesus say this stone would do?

    Read Luke 20:18. Give your interpretation of this verse:

    What made the leaders want to kill Jesus at this point? (Mark 12:12)

9. How did the Pharisees and Herodians attempt to flatter Jesus in verse 14?

    What made this question a controversial one?

    Did these two parties agree?

    Share Jesus' answer:

    What does this mean in your life?

    How did the Apostle Paul expound on this principle of the Lord's? (See Romans 13:1-7, also consider 1 Peter 2:13-17)

10. Read the hypothetical situation the Sadducees gave to Jesus in verses 18-23.

What made this grotesque story even more offensive coming from them? (v.18)

What were they trying to do?

To which law were they actually referring?
Summarize Deuteronomy 25:5-10:

11. How did Jesus correct their errors:

    a.) In regard to marriage? (See v.25; Luke 20:35)

    For which lifetime is marriage given? (See 1 Corinthians 7:31-33)

    What will happen to us at the resurrection?
    (See I Corinthians 15:44-52)

    b.) In regard to the resurrection of the dead? (See v. 26- 27)

        See also:

        Psalm 49:15:

        Psalm 73:24:

        Job 19:25-26:

        John 5:25-29:

12. Read verses 28-34. What is the greatest commandment?

And the next most important?

How are you obeying and applying these commandments in your life?

13. How did the scribe reply? (v.33)

    What is the significance of mentioning the burnt offerings and sacrifices? Use the following to answer:

    1 Samuel 15:22:

    Psalm 51:16-17:

    Isaiah 64:6:

    Hosea 6:6:

    Micah 6:6-8:

14. Carefully study Jesus' questions to the people in v.35-37.

    What is the answer?

    Summarize these verses:

    2 Samuel 7:12-16:

    Romans 1:3:

Psalm 110:1:

Hebrews 1:2,5,8:

15. As opposed to the rulers, how did the common people receive Jesus' teaching? (v.37)

Give your opinion: Is this still the case today? (Refer to James 2:5-7)

16. In verses 38-40, how did Jesus warn the people about the scribes? (Also see Matthew 6:2-5)

What was their sin?
(Also see Matthew 23:13-15)

What would they receive from the Hand of God? (v.40)

How are ministers to serve? (See 1 Peter 5:2-3)

Pray for your pastors his week!

17. What was Jesus doing watching the treasury? (v.41)

Who only has a right to do this?

Is the amount we give of importance to God?
(v.41-42; 2 Corinthians 8:12)
What *is* important?

Answer using the following verses:
1 Samuel 2:3b:

2 Corinthians 8:1-7; 9:7:

Matthew 23:23:

18. How much did the widow really give?

Lord, we thank you for the example of this widow who was able to give all she had because she had already given herself to you!
May we, and all that we have, be entirely yours, as we commit all to you today.

Lesson Eighteen: Mark 13

> "For nation will rise against nation, and kingdom against kingdom. And there will be famines, pestilences, and earthquakes in various places. All these are the beginning of sorrows."
> - Matthew 24:7-8

> "Then the sign of the Son of Man will appear in heaven, and all the tribes of the earth will mourn, and they will see the Son of Man coming on the clouds of heaven with power and great glory."
> - Matthew 24:30

> "And what I say to you, I say to all: Watch!"
> - Mark 13:37

In Mark 13, we have an abbreviated version of Jesus' prophecy concerning the end times. (For reference, see Matthew 24.) As with many Bible prophecies, we can see a double interpretation- Jesus speaks not only of the destruction of Jerusalem and the end of the national life of Israel, but of the great tribulation to befall the entire earth, and His second coming in glory.

In 70 A.D., the Roman general Titus and his forces came into Jerusalem to put down a Jewish rebellion with such incredible violence and hatred, that, as Jesus had said 40 years earlier, not one stone was left upon another: the magnificent temple was laid even with the ground! More than one million, three hundred fifty thousand were put to death in the siege of Jerusalem. It was because of the Passover, that more than three million people were assembled there at the time. Famine accompanied the siege and so much blood ran that fires were put out.[40] Truly, the curse that the Jews called down upon themselves at Jesus' crucifixion, "Let His blood be on us, and on our children"[41] came to pass within one generation.

The message Jesus had for Peter, Andrew, James, and John was one of persecution for their testimony for Him, as well as a warning not to be deceived by false Christ. He also assured them of the continued presence of His Holy Spirit, which would "give them a mouth and wisdom, which all your

---

[40] Josephus, *Jewish Wars*, Vol. VI.
[41] Matthew 27:25

adversaries will not be able to gainsay or resist."[42] Jesus' admonition to the disciples is the same for us': Watch and pray!

Since the second interpretation of Jesus' prophecy has not yet been fulfilled, and could take place in our lifetime, should the Christian be fearful of the Great Tribulation? Emphatically, No! For, "the Lord knows how to deliver the godly out of temptations and to reserve the unjust under punishment for the day of judgment."[43] 1 Thessalonians 1:10 tells us that Jesus "delivers us from the wrath to come" and 1 Thessalonians 5:9 assures us that "God did not appoint us to wrath." At the end of the current church age, Jesus will meet us in the clouds of heaven, and everyone who has trusted Christ as Savior, living or dead, will be taken to be with Him, and "so shall we ever be with the Lord."[44] Immediately afterward the Tribulation period will begin on the earth, which will be seven years of unparalleled wickedness, with the Antichrist "who opposes and exalts himself above all that is called God ... sits as God in the temple of God, showing himself that he is God."[45]

This period of persecution, martyrdom, judgment, and physical upheaval upon the earth will end with the Second Coming of Christ. We believers will accompany Him in the armies of heaven, and participate in the battle that will see the complete overthrow of Satan and his minions, the Antichrist and the False Prophet.

Christians are told to watch for the signs of these events, that we may be ready for the coming of our Lord. Why is end time prophecy given? That it might affect the way we live our lives today. 2 Peter 3:10-14 puts it this way:

> "But the day of the Lord will come as a thief in the night, in which the heavens will pass away with a great noise, and the elements melt with fervent heat; both the earth and the works that are in it will be burned up. Therefore, since all of these things will be dissolved, what manner of persons ought you to be in holy conduct and godliness, looking for and hastening the coming of the day of God, because of which the heavens will be dissolved being on fire, and the elements will melt with fervent heat? Nevertheless we, according to His promise, look for new heavens and a new earth in which

---

[42] Luke 21:15
[43] 2 Peter 2:9
[44] 1 Thessalonians 4:17
[45] 2 Thessalonians 2:4

righteousness dwells. Therefore, beloved, looking forward to these things, be diligent to be found by Him in peace, without spot and blameless."

Read Mark 13

Please **pray** for the guidance of the Holy Spirit before answering the questions.

1. Discuss the temple at Jerusalem, using these scriptures:

    John 2:20:

    Luke 21:5:

    Luke 2:21-22,27:

    Matthew 4:5,6:

    What attitude did the Jews have toward the Temple?

    Describe what happened to the Temple at the moment of Jesus' death. (Refer to Matthew 27:50-55; Mark 15:37,38)

2. What did Jesus say would happen to the Temple? (v.2)

    Read these prophecies:

    Daniel 11:30-31

    Micah 3:9-12

3. Write the two questions which Peter, James, John, and Andrew asked Jesus. (v.4)

   How did Jesus warn them in verse 5?

   Read Jeremiah 29:8

4. Are Christians supposed to be gullible?
   Refer to Luke 16:8b and Matthew 10:16 to answer.

   Where should we get our wisdom?
   Answer based on the following:

   John 14:26:

   1 Corinthians 2:6-16:

   Ephesians 4:11-13:

   Ephesians 5:15-17:

   Are you known as a woman of wisdom?

5. What claim would these deceivers make? (v.6)

   Did this happen?

   Answer based on Acts 5:36-37; 8:9-10

   Has this happened in recent years? Give particulars if you can.

6. Which rumors and happenings should not trouble us? (v.7)

   Should a Christian be troubled anyway?

   Write these scriptures.

   John 14:1-3:

   John 16:33:

   Romans 8:31-34:

   Philippians 4:6-7:

7. Which signs should we look for in the end times? (v.8)

   Are we in the end times now?

   Read Hebrews 1:2 and offer evidence from current events as well.

8. Describe the persecutions that the apostles would face. (v.9-13)

   Also summarize these passages:

   Acts 4:5-13:

   How does Acts 4:13 confirm Mark 13:11?

   Acts 5:27-33, 40-41:

Acts 6:8-15:

Acts 7:54-60:

2 Timothy 3:10-12 (Paul):

Have you been persecuted for your faith?

9. In verse 14, Jesus begins to speak of the Great Tribulation. What is the "Abomination of desolation"? Answer using the following:

    2 Thessalonians 2:3-4:

    Daniel 7:25:

    Daniel 9:27, 12:11:

    Revelation 13:14:

10. How does Jesus describe the Great Tribulation period, as well as warn those who are living in that time? (v.14-20)

    Will Christians be involved in these events?

    Answer after reading these scriptures:

    1 Thessalonians 4:16-17

    1 Thessalonians 5:9

2 Thessalonians 2:1-3

1 Corinthians 15:51-52

John 14:1-3

11. How do we see God's mercy in verse 20?

   Who are "the elect" of those days?

   Answer after reading the following:

   Romans 9:27-28

   Romans 11:26-29

   Revelation 7:3-8

   Revelation 14:1-4

12. In verses 21-22, whom is Christ describing?

   Refer to 1 John 2:18, Revelation 13:1-13; 19:20 for additional information.

13. Describe the earth's conditions preceding the Second Coming of Christ in verses 24-25.

   Also see:

Zephaniah 1:14-15:

Isaiah 13:9-10:

Isaiah 34:4:

14. How will Jesus return? (v.26)

    Also see:

    Revelation 1:7:

    Mark 14:62:

15. How did Jesus ascend to the Father?
    (See Acts 1:9-11)

    How will He come for His church?
    (See 1 Thessalonians 4:17)

16. What will Jesus do at His return? (v.27)

    Summarize Matthew 25:31-34,41,46

17. What can we learn from the parable of the fig tree? (v.28-30)

18. Use these scriptures to expound on verse 31:

    Hebrews 1:10-12:

2 Peter 3:10:

Psalm 119:89:

19. Read verses 32-37. Why are we told to watch?

What is our attitude and manner of life to be as we watch and wait? (See Luke 12:35-44)

Dear Lord Jesus, we pray that we might be found faithful stewards, redeeming the time, and waiting upon you in prayer! Praise you, Lord, that You are coming for us soon!
"Even so, come Lord Jesus!"

Lesson Nineteen: Mark 14:1-26

> "She has done what she could; she has come beforehand to anoint My body for burial."
>
> \- Mark 14:8

> "And he took bread, gave thanks and broke it, and gave it to them, saying, 'This is my body which is given for you; do this in remembrance of me'. Likewise He also took the cup after supper, saying, 'This cup is the new covenant in My blood, which is shed for you.'"
>
> \- Luke 22:19-20

> "I am the living bread which came down from heaven. If anyone eats of this bread, he will live forever; and the bread that I shall give is My flesh, which I shall give for the life of the world."
>
> \- John 6:51

> "For as often as you eat this bread and drink this cup, you proclaim the Lord's death till He comes."
>
> \- 1 Corinthians 11:26

In Mark 14, we move rapidly now through the events which will lead to the arrest, trial, and crucifixion of Jesus, the most significant event in the history of the human race.

I cannot help but ponder the emotional states of mind of those who were to be participants in the events of the last earthly days of our Savior: the chief priests and scribes, grimly determined to kill Jesus, seeking a discreet way to arrest Him, and absolutely, malevolently glad at the traitorous offer of Judas. Consider Judas himself, the treasurer, the thief, a man so covetous, so possessed by Satan[46] that he sold Jesus and his own soul - for thirty pieces of silver! Think of Mary, whose last sacrificed act of worship, the anointing of Jesus with spikenard, has indeed become a memorial of devotion and love throughout twenty centuries, just as Jesus said it would. And how can we describe the emotions of the disciples at the Last Supper? They had been told repeatedly by the Lord of His coming arrest, trial, and crucifixion, but had tried not to believe it. When Jesus told them that He

---

[46] Luke 22:3

would not partake of the Passover cup with them again, (therefore He greatly desired to share it with them that night before He suffered[47]), what a mixture of dread, fear, and sorrow must have been theirs! Even though Jesus spoke of His resurrection as well, the sorrow caused by His impending death overwhelmed those men, and the thought that one of their number would betray Jesus was more than they could bear.

Whenever I read of the events of the last week of Jesus' life in any of the gospel accounts, my heart is flooded with many emotions. I feel dread, for I know what Jesus suffered - the treachery, the humiliation, the pain, the agony of separation from the Father. I'm angered
at Judas, the chief priests, and cowardly Pilate, even though their infamous actions were part of the outworking of God's eternal plan. I sorrow deeply for my sin that put Him on the cross. I feel reverence and awe that God Himself walked here among us, never wavering from the plan of salvation determined from the foundation of the world. I rejoice that now I have eternal life, and that at any time I could go to be with Him, and see my Lord face to face!

As our study in the Book of Mark begins to draw to a close, meditate on these things. What does Jesus' death mean to you? Determine this week to know one thing: "Jesus Christ and Him crucified."[48]

Read Mark 14:1-26

Please **pray** for the help of the Holy Spirit before answering the questions.

1. Describe the feast that was taking place at this point in Jesus' life. (v.1)

    Read Exodus 12:1-20, and find as many symbols of Christ as you can. (Also refer to 1 Corinthians 5:7)

2. What were the chief priests and scribes seeking to do? (v.1)

    Would they have admitted this? (See John 7:19,20)

---

[47] Luke 22:15
[48] 1 Corinthians 2:2

What was their dilemma? (v.2)

Why might there be an uproar of the people?

Write the answers found in these Scriptures:

Matthew 9:35-36:

John 8:37-40:

Mark 12:37b:

John 12:12-19:

Also research these verses:

Exodus 23:17:

Psalm 42:4:

Ezra 6:16-20:

Luke 2:41-42:

John 2:13,23:

3. Read v.3. What more do we know about this dinner from another gospel? (See John 12:1-3)

How did Mary worship Jesus? (v.3)

Research the meaning and uses of anointing oil:

Exodus 30:22-30:

I Samuel 16:1,12-13:

How is Jesus represented in both of these examples?

4. Discuss the worship of our Lord, using these scriptures:

Psalm 118:19:

Psalm 133:1-2:

Isaiah 66:1-2:

Habakkuk 2:20:

John 4:21-24:

Acts 2:4, 8-11:

Romans 12:1:

1 Corinthians 14:15:

How have you determined that you will worship the Lord this week?

5. What objection was made to Mary's sacrificial gift? (v.4-5)

   Who actually led the indignant protest, and why? (John 12:4-6)

   Describe the sin of covetousness:

   Job 31:24,25,28:

   Psalm 10:3:

   Psalm 119:36:

   What did this sin lead Judas to do? (v.10-11)

   Refer to Matthew 26:14-16 and Jeremiah 22:17 to answer:

6. Jesus was pleased with Mary's gift. Recount His answer in verses 6-9.

   How are you helping the poor?

   What is the significance of verse 8 to you?

   At which other occasion was Jesus given burial spices?
   (See Matthew 2:1-2,10-11)

   How do these things reveal the eternal plan of God?
   Answer using the following:

2 Timothy 1:9:

1 Peter 1:19-20:

Revelation 13:8:

7. Describe the arrangements Christ had made for their Passover supper. (v.12-16; also Luke 22:7-13; Matthew 26:17-19)

   Which characteristics do you see of our Lord in these arrangements? Give supporting scriptures!

8. Describe Jesus' emotions as He sat at the Passover Supper with His disciples:

   Luke 22:15:

   John 13:1, 21a:

   How He loves you and me!

9. What was Jesus' shocking statement in verse 18?

   How was this prophesied?

   Zechariah 11:12b:

   John 6:70-71:

Read Psalm 41:9

How does this Psalm identify Judas? (Also refer to John 13:26-27)

10. How did the other disciples show their candidness and transparency? (v.19)

*Do you ever betray the Lord by your attitude, lifestyle, prayerlessness, not witnessing, or by taking Him for granted?
As the disciples did, ask Him, "Lord, is it I?"*

11. Describe the curse put upon Judas in verse 21. (See Psalm 109:5-8)

Did this curse come to pass?

(Refer to Matthew 27:3-10; Acts 1:15-20)

12. Read verses 22-25, Matthew 26:26-29 and Luke 22:17-20. What new feast did our Lord institute that night?

What are we told to do? (Luke 22:19; 1 Corinthians 11:26)

13. Give the significance of the bread and the cup, using Luke 22:19-20; John 6:48-51;53-58.

14. Read verse 24 carefully. What also was established for us? (Also refer to Hebrews 8:6,7,13)

15. When will Jesus drink again of the fruit of the vine? (v.25; Revelation 19:7-9)

16. The hymns Jesus sang with His disciples were from *The Great Hallel*, Psalms 113-118.

Read the psalms and sing your favorite verses to the Lord this week!

Dearest Lord, may our praise to you be acceptable in your sight!

Lesson Twenty: Mark 14:27-52

> "I gave my back to those who struck me, and my cheeks to those who plucked out the beard; I did not hide my face from shame and spitting."
>
> - Isaiah 50:6

> "All we like sheep have gone astray; we have turned, every one, to his way; and the Lord has laid upon Him the iniquity of us all. He was oppressed and He was afflicted, yet He opened not His mouth; He was led as a lamb to the slaughter, and as a sheep before its shearers is silent, so He opened not His mouth."
>
> - Isaiah 53:6-7

> "And the Lord turned and looked at Peter. And Peter remembered the word of the Lord, how He had said to him, 'Before the rooster crows, you will deny me three times.' Then Peter went out and wept bitterly."
>
> - Luke 22:61-62

> "And all things are of God, who has reconciled us to Himself by Jesus Christ... God was in Christ, reconciling the world unto Himself, not inputting their trespasses unto them; and has committed unto us the word of reconciliation."
>
> - 2 Corinthians 5:18-19

As Jesus had stated earlier in the Garden of Gethsemane, it was truly Satan's hour, the hour of triumph for the powers of darkness.[49] From His betrayal, His arrest (as if He were a dangerous criminal) to the kangaroo court proceedings He was subjected to, we can see the limitless wickedness of man. Greed, envy, falsehood, duplicity, blasphemy, and violence were the prevailing characteristics of this hate-filled night. How true Jesus' words in John 8:44 were proven to be in regard to the religious rulers, for He said, "You are of your father the devil, and the lusts of your father you will do. He was a murderer from the beginning, and abode not in the truth, because there is no truth in him."

---

[49] Mark 14:53

The high priest asked Jesus point-blank, "Are you the Christ, the son of the Blessed?" When Jesus replied, "I am," all the fury of hell broke loose. The high priest, in a strictly unlawful act, tore his clothes and cried, "Blasphemy!" The officers cursed, reviled and spit on Jesus, contemptuously defying Him to prophesy who hit Him. They cried blasphemy, yet they were the ones guilty of blasphemy against the name of God- God the Son, the very One who came to save His people from their sins! The decision was made: condemn Him to death. Ostensibly, it was the rulers' evil decision that sent Jesus to the cross; but it was God's eternal plan that His death would mean life to the world.

Meanwhile, in the courtyard, one of the saddest (and most instructive) incidents in all of scripture took place: Peter's denial of Christ. Jesus had warned Peter at the last supper that Satan desired to sift him as wheat, but that He was praying that Peter's faith would not fail.[50] As they went to the Mount of Olives, Jesus told Peter of his upcoming denial. Peter, ever confident in his flesh, refused to believe his Master. When Peter denied Jesus, every laudable quality of his character- courage, faith, loyalty, integrity- failed him in this hour of supreme testing. Are you trusting in your natural abilities and strong character to save you; or see you through when the test comes?

These things will fail you every time, for "all our righteousness are as filthy rags."[51] Apart from Christ, we are utterly unclean. We can only fail the Lord, and we will find ourselves, like Peter, weeping in bitter despair. Luke tells us that Jesus glanced at Peter as the rooster crowed, at the moment of His denial. In this glance I see not only sorrow, but tenderness and forgiveness as well. Peter would later accept that forgiveness, and be honored as a leader of the Christian Church after the resurrection, preaching salvation to thousands on the day of Pentecost, eventually dying as a martyr for his Lord.

There was also forgiveness in Jesus for those who mocked and tormented Him, as well as for those who put Him on the cross. Did they accept this forgiveness? One day we will know. But most importantly, there is forgiveness for you in Christ--will you accept it, and be saved?

---

[50] Luke 22:31-32
[51] Isaiah 64:6

Read Mark 14:53-72

Please **pray** for the guidance of the Holy Spirit before you answer the questions.

1. Describe the gathering that awaited Jesus. (v.53)

    How was justice to be carried out, according to the Law? Summarize the following:

    Exodus 23:1-7:

    Leviticus 19:11-16:

    Deuteronomy 1:15-17:

    Deuteronomy 17:8-11:

    Deuteronomy 19:16-19:

    2 Chronicles 19:5-10:

2. Yet, what was being done in the trial of Jesus that night? (v.55-56)

    Read and reflect on these verses:

    Proverbs 6:16-19:

    Proverbs 18:5:

Ecclesiastes 3:16-17:

Isaiah 59:14

Prophetic verses:

Psalm 27:12:

Psalm 35:11:

3. What was the testimony of the false witnesses? (v.57-58)

   What had Jesus actually been referring to? (See John 2:19-21)

   Read verse 59. Did the chief priests actually have a case against our Lord?
   Use their own laws to prove your answer!

4. How did Jesus respond to this provocation? (v. 60)
   (See Matthew 26:63; Isaiah 53:7)

5. The high priest finally confronted Jesus with an actual issue. (v.61)
   What was it?

   Had this controversy come up before?

   Summarize the following passages:

   John 8:53-59:

John 10:24-33:

6. What was Jesus' answer? (v.62)
   (See also Matthew 26:64; Luke 22:70)

   Who is Jesus Christ to you?

7. What is meant by the phrase "sitting at the right hand of the Power?"

   Exodus 15:6:

   Psalm 80:17:

   Psalm 110:1:

   Romans 8:34:

   Hebrews 1:1-3:

   Psalm 118:16:

   Ephesians 1:20:

   1 Peter 3:22:

8. Do we read of Jesus "coming in the clouds of heaven" elsewhere? Write these:

   Matthew 24:29-30:

Acts 1:9-11:

Revelation 1:7:

9. Describe the high priest's reaction in verse 63.

What did this signify?

Joshua 7:6:

2 Samuel 1:11-12:

Esther 4:1-3:

Was it legal for the High Priest to tear his clothing?

Leviticus 10:6a:

Leviticus 21:10:

10. What was the charge against Jesus? (v.64)

The sentence?

Review these verses:

Leviticus 24:16

John 5:18

John 19:7

11. What was the supreme irony concerning Jesus' accusers?
    (See Matthew 12:31-32; Psalm 102:25-27; Hebrews 1:8-10)

12. How did the officers and servants of the priest treat Jesus? (v. 65)

   How was this prophesied?

   Psalm 2:2:

   Isaiah 50:6:

   Isaiah 53:4:

   John 15:24:

Our Savior suffered thus for you and me -- praise and worship Him today!

13. Read verses 66-72, and recount the story of Peter's denial.

   What lessons can we learn in regard to our own walks with the Lord?

   Read and summarize:

   Mark 14:38:

Romans 7:18:

Romans 12:3:

1 Corinthians 10:11-12:

Galatians 6:3:

Dear Lord, help us to remember and practice 2 Corinthians 3:5: "Not that we are sufficient of ourselves to think of anything as being from ourselves, but our sufficiency is of God."

Lesson Twenty-One: Mark 15:1-24

> "The scepter shall not depart from Judah, nor a lawgiver from between his feet, until Shiloh comes; and to Him shall be the obedience of the people."
>
> - Genesis 49:10

> "My kingdom is not of this world. If my kingdom were of this world, My servants would fight, so that I should not be delivered unto the Jews; but now My kingdom is not from here ... You say rightly that I am a king. For this cause I was born, and for this cause I have come into the world... "
>
> - John 18:36-37

> "He was oppressed and He was afflicted, yet He opened not His mouth; He was led as a lamb to the slaughter, and as a sheep before its shearers is silent, so He opened not His mouth."
>
> - Isaiah 53:7

> "A double minded man is unstable in all his ways."
>
> - James 1: 8

In the trial of Jesus before Pontius Pilate, we see the most shocking miscarriage of justice the world has ever known. Yet God allowed this vacillating, self-serving Roman politician a role in putting to death the Lord of Glory, even though Pilate cared little for the charges brought against Him, and repeatedly stated, "I find no fault in Him."[52]

As we recall from Mark 14, the Jews had condemned Jesus to death on a charge of blasphemy. Why, then, must they appeal to the Roman governor? Incredibly, Genesis 49:10 (the prophecy given by Jacob in blessing his son Judah approximately 1800 years earlier) tells us why. God promised His people that there would always be a "lawgiver," or king from the tribe of Judah - that "the scepter would not depart from him."[53] A king, by definition, has absolute power, including the power of life and death, over his people. At the time "Shiloh", (Messiah) was among His people, Israel was subjugated

---
[52] John 18:38; 19:4,6
[53] 2 Samuel 2:4; 7:12-16; Psalm 89:20-37

under the iron fist of Rome. They were without a king, and without the power to execute the death sentence upon those whom they condemned. Thus John 18:31: "Then Pilate said to them, 'You take Him and judge Him according to your law.' Therefore the Jews said to him, 'It is not lawful for us to put anyone to death.'"

In order for the Romans to sentence and execute Jesus, there had to be a charge brought of sedition against their government, which the Jews attempted. But Pilate knew that envy was the motive of these false accusations. Matthew 27:24 tells us that Pilate tried to release Jesus, and then washed his hands before the multitude saying, "I am innocent of the blood of this just person. You see to it." To which the people replied, "His blood be on us and on our children." And so the blood of Jesus has been on the Jewish people ever since, as history, from the destruction of Jerusalem to the persecutions of this century, has borne it out.

But was Pilate really innocent in this matter of "the king of the Jews"? I think not! In God's universe, with its absolutes of right and wrong, one cannot declare oneself innocent, abandon all responsibility, and allow injustice to take place. If Pilate had been a man of courage and conviction, he would never have given in to the mobs crying, "Crucify Him!" History tells us that miserable Pilate, like Judas Iscariot before him, took his own life. Both had been instrumental in condemning the innocent; both came to a violent end.

Let us remember that, even though Isaiah 53:10 says, "It pleased the Lord to bruise Him and to make His soul an offering for sin." God is not mocked. Whatsoever a man sows, that shall he also reap. [54]

Read Mark 15:1-24

Please **pray** for the guidance of the Holy Spirit before answering the questions.

    1. Where was Jesus taken? (v.1)

---

[54] Galatians 6:7

Why? (See John 18:31)

How did this circumstance fulfill the prophecy Jesus had given? (Refer to Matthew 20:18-19)

2. In order to have a charge against Jesus that Pilate would pay attention to, what lie did the Jews tell Pilate? (See Luke 23:2)

What had Jesus actually said about paying tribute to Caesar? (See Mark 12:14-17)

3. What did Jesus' answer to Pilate's question in verse 2 mean?

Write these verses:

    Psalm 45:6-7:

    Hebrews 1:8-9:

    Isaiah 9:6-7:

    Jeremiah 23:5:

    Daniel 2:44:

    Micah 5:2:

    Zechariah 6:13:

Matthew 2:2:

John 19:19-20:

Revelation 19:11-16:

What does Christ's kingship mean to you?

4. Turn to the Crucifixion story in Luke 23 and read verses 5-12.

Who did Pilate send Jesus to, in an attempt to escape responsibility?

What twisted enjoyment did Herod get out of seeing Jesus? (Luke 23:8; Matthew 14:1; Luke 9:7-9)

Describe the mocking Herod and his men gave to Jesus in Luke 23:11.

How was this unlikely friendship between Pilate and Herod prophesied?

Summarize Psalm 2:

5. Return to Mark 15. Why did Pilate marvel at Jesus in v.3-5?

Also refer to these verses:

Isaiah 53:7:

1 Peter 2:21-23:

How should a Christian react to accusations? (Psalm 35:1)
*Ask yourself, "Am I too quick to jump to my own defense?"
Keep in mind Job 9:20!*

6. Did Pilate find any fault in Jesus? (See John 18-:38)

   In John 18:39, which custom did Pilate attempt to invoke in order to free Jesus? (Also see Mark 15:6)

7. Describe the other notable prisoner. (v. 7)

   What did the multitude begin to demand? (v.8)

   Which prisoner did Pilate assume the people would want freed? (v.9)

   Why? (v.10; John 11:47; John 12:19)

   *Are you envying someone today? If so, read
   Proverbs 14:30, 1 Corinthians 3:3, and James 5:9!*

8. How did the chief priests move the people? (v. 11-13)
   (Refer to Acts 3:13-15)

9. Jesus took the place and punishment that Barabbas deserved. What is the spiritual significance of this in your life?

10. Did Pilate make another attempt to free Jesus? (v.14)
    (See also Matthew 27:19)

How did the Jews attempt to bully Pilate? (v.12)

Were they successful?

In your opinion, what kind of person was Pilate?

Are you a person who stands for your convictions?

11. As Pilate made one more attempt to release Jesus, what did the Jews tell him?

    Read Matthew 27:24-25 and Luke 23:28-30.

    Has this curse they called upon themselves taken place?

12. What season was it at the time of the crucifixion? (John 19:14)

    Give the significance of God's timing from these verses:

    Exodus 12:5-11:

    John 1:29:

    1 Corinthians 5:7b:

13. How was Jesus punished before His crucifixion? (v.15)
    Was this in any way justified? (See John 18:38)

Who else was mistreated this way by the Jews?
(See Acts 5:27-29,40; 2 Corinthians 11:24)

What was Paul's conclusion in 2 Corinthians 12:10, that should be our attitude also?

14. Read verses 16-20. Describe the mocking Jesus received.

    Read and reflect on Psalm 69:20:

    What are we as Christians warned in 2 Timothy 3:12?

    Have you suffered mocking for your stand for Christ?

15. Who was compelled to carry the cross for Jesus?

    How did his son evince a godly heritage later on in the early church?
    See Romans 16:13

    Let us consider the example we are being to our children!

16. What was the meaning of the place of crucifixion? (v.22)

    What was offered Jesus to drink? (v.23)

    Read John 9:23-24 and Mark 15:24. Describe what took place.

    Where were these actions prophesied?

Dana Kruckenberg Thompson

Dearest Lord, it breaks our hearts to see the treatment You endured for us, but we know that you endured the cross, and despised the shame for the joy that was set before you - our salvation. Thank You, Jesus!

Lesson Twenty-Two: Mark 15:25-47

"Now it was the third hour, and they crucified Him."
- Mark 15:25

"... He said, 'It is finished.'"
- John 19:30

"For He made Him who knew no sin to be sin for us,
that we might become the righteousness of God in Him."
- 2 Corinthians 5:21

Jesus had endured the mocking, spitting, and whipping, having been beaten beyond recognition, when the hour of crucifixion finally took place. The Romans had designed this form of execution to provide the most painful, lingering agony possible, with death eventually coming about when the weakened victim could no longer draw up his lungs for air. Crucifixion was the mode of execution for slaves and the most wretched criminals. Our Lord died a despicable cursed death, for even the Hebrew scriptures state, "Cursed is everyone who hangs on a tree."[55]

When I consider the human element of the crucifixion - the sheer hatefulness of Jesus' accusers and tormentors - I feel an indescribable sorrow and heaviness in my heart for the depths of sin men can sink to. But when I consider the heavenly, God-ordained element of the same scene, my heart is lifted with joy unspeakable, for I know that there is no sin so deep, that Jesus' atonement on the cross cannot pay for; no person so wicked but that he might come to the cross for salvation and new birth!

Jesus drew His last breath and cried, "It is finished." Because of His death, our new life in Him began. Please do not reject so great a salvation! Let not Christ's death be in vain. He died for you - live for Him.

---

[55] Deuteronomy 21:23

Read Mark 15:25-47

Please **pray** for the guidance of the Holy Spirit before you begin answering the questions.

1. What took place at the third hour?
   Describe the emotion that the crucifixion stirs in your heart.

2. How was death by crucifixion regarded?
   By the Jews:

   Deuteronomy 21:22-23:

   Galatians 3:13:

   Psalm 69:19:

   By the Romans:

   Psalm 22:6:

   Luke 23: 19,25:

   Philippians 2:5-8:

3. According to His accusers, what did the inscription over Jesus' cross say? (v. 26; Luke 23:2,38)

   How did the priests' objection in John 19:21 show their unrelenting malice?

Did the inscription remain? (John 19:22)

Prove from these scriptures that Jesus is the King of the Jews.

    Numbers 24:17:

    Isaiah 9:6-7:

    Psalm 118: 25-26:

    Isaiah 33:22:

    Daniel 9:25:

    Micah 5:2:

    Zechariah 9:9:

    Matthew 2:2,6:

    Matthew 27:11:

4. Additionally and ultimately, who does scripture say Jesus is?

    Psalm 2:6-7:

    Romans 9:5; 14:9:

Philippians 2:9-11:

1 Timothy 6:15:

Revelation 11:15:

5. Who was crucified on either side of Jesus? (v.27-28)

How was this prophesied? (Isaiah 53:12)

Read the account of the two thieves in Luke 23:39-43.

How did one of them demonstrate repentance? (Hebrews 7:25)

Did God honor his request to be remembered in Christ's kingdom?

Is anyone too evil to be saved? Give scriptures!

6. In verses 29-32, what were the insults hurled at Jesus?
(See also Matthew 27:43)

7. Look up these verses to see God's faithfulness in fulfilling prophecy:

Psalm 22:6-8,16:

Psalm 69:7,19:

Psalm 109:25:

John 2:19-22:

8. Could Jesus have saved himself?

   Psalm 2:

   Psalm 110:1-6:

   Philippians 2:9-11:

   Revelation 19:11-16:

9. Why then, did He endure the mocking and scourging, as well as His torturous death?

   Hebrews 5:5-9:

   1 John 3:8:

   Isaiah 53:8-11:

   Acts 17:2-3:

   Hebrews 9:12-15:

   Hebrews 12:2-3:

   1 Peter 1:10-11:

10. What happened in the sixth to the ninth hour? (v. 33)

How was this prophesied?
(See Amos 8:9)

Describe other times when God has (or will) manifest signs in the heavens to show His ultimate sovereignty:

Genesis 19:24-25,28:

Exodus 19:16-19:

Joshua 10:12-14:

Zephaniah 1:14-15:

Mark 13: 24-26:

Revelation 6:12-17:

Write some examples of your own from scripture!

11. What did Jesus cry out in verse 34?

Write Psalm 22:1:

Had God the Father actually forsaken Jesus?
Regarding the Father:

Psalm 145:17:

Psalm 5:4:

Habakkuk 1:13a:

Regarding the Son:

Romans 15:3:

2 Corinthians 5:21:

Galatians 3:13:

Why then, might Jesus have cried out these words?
(Luke 4:13; John 14:30)

*Describe a time when you felt forsaken by God,
and how He ministered to you.*

12. Describe what was said and done in verses 35-36.
    Refer to Psalm 69:19-21

*How does the realization of Christ's suffering affect your walk with Him
today?*

13. Does Elijah have a place in end times prophecy?
    Review these scriptures:

    Malachi 4:5:

    Revelation 11:3-12:

James 5:17-18:

14. Tell the events that took place as Jesus breathed His last. (v.37-38; Matthew 27:51-54)

    Did He die as other humans die? (John 10:17-18)

15. What was the veil that tore? (Exodus 26:31-34)

    What spiritual significance is there in the splitting of the veil?

    Ephesians 2:13-14:

    Hebrews 6:19-20:

    Hebrews 10:19,-20:

16. What effect did Christ's manner of death have on the centurion? (v.39)

    Did this man take the first step toward salvation?
    See Romans 10:9,13 and John 20:31.

17. Name the women who remained at the scene of the crucifixion. (v.40-41)

    Meanwhile, where were Jesus' disciples?(Mark 14:50)

The Name of Jesus Christ is cursed and reviled everywhere today. When this happens, what kind of follower of Jesus are you?

18. Read verse 42-47, and John 19:31-37. Why did the Jews want the crucified men's legs broken?

    How was prophecy fulfilled?
    Refer to the following:

    Psalm 34:20:

    Zechariah 12:10:

19. Who came forward for the body of Jesus? (v.43; John 19:38)

    Tell more about the "need" for Joseph to be a secret follower of Jesus.
    Refer to John 9:22; 16:2:

    Yet, what does Jesus tell us in Matthew 10:32?

20. Read verses 46-47, as well as Matthew 27:59-61 and John 19:39-42.

    What kind of tomb was Jesus laid in by Joseph and Nicodemus? (Refer to Isaiah 53:9)

21. Compare John 19:41 with Matthew 1:22-23 and explain the spiritual significance of these verses in your own words.

Dearest Lord, We thank you for showing us in Your Word the perfect work that You accomplished in the life of your Son Jesus. We take comfort in knowing that there is nothing that can take place in our lives which You do not already see as perfected!

Lesson Twenty-Three: Mark 16

"He is risen!"

- Mark 16:6

"Therefore my heart is glad and my glory rejoices: My flesh also shall rest in hope. For thou will not leave my soul in will thou suffer thine Holy One to see corruption."

- Psalm 16:9-10

"I am He who lives and was dead, and behold, I am alive forevermore. Amen."

- Revelation 1:18

"Because I live, you shall live also."

- John 14:19

Truly, the most thrilling words ever uttered in the history of mankind are contained in our final chapter of the Book of Mark: "He is risen!" On this statement of historical fact rests the fate of the entire human race; on the response of each person to the resurrection of Jesus Christ hangs their eternal destiny!

The resurrection of Christ along with His deity, pre-existence, and virgin birth, is the central fact of the Christian faith. Jesus never spoke of His death without also speaking of His resurrection.[56] His rising from the dead was prophesied in the Old Testament.[57]

The resurrection of Jesus was the text of every sermon preached in the early church as recorded in the book of Acts. Indeed, it was this fact that the apostles declared in order to prove that Jesus is the Christ.[58] Belief in this doctrine is essential to salvation. Romans 10:9 tells us that "If you confess with your mouth the Lord Jesus and believe in your heart that God has raised Him from the dead, you shall be saved."

---

[56] Matthew 20:18-19; Mark 10:33-34; Luke 18:32-33; John 10:17-18
[57] Job 19:25-26; Psalm 16:10; Psalm 17:15; Isaiah 25:6
[58] Acts 2:22-32; 3:26; 4:10; 13:26-37; Acts 17:1-3, 30-31; Acts 26

THE GOSPEL ACCORDING TO MARK: A Walk in the Word

To the Christian, the resurrection is our living hope of an inheritance incorruptible and undefiled, reserved in heaven for us. Because He lives, we live. We have assurance from John 11:25:
"I am the resurrection and the life. He who believes in Me, though he may die, he shall live." Praise God!

Let us close our devotional thoughts on the book of Mark with the words of this hymn:

> *"Because He lives, I can face tomorrow,*
> *Because He lives, all fear is gone.*
> *Because I know Who holds the future,*
> *And life is worth the living,*
> *Just because He lives."*

Read Mark 16

Please **pray** for the guidance of the Holy Spirit before you answer the questions.

1. Who went to anoint the body of Jesus?

   Had Jesus referred to this anointing before?
   (See John 12:3; Mark 14:8)

2. What question did the women ask among themselves in verse 3?

   How was that question answered? (v.4)

3. Why had there been a stone at the opening to the cave?
   (See Matthew 27:62-66)

   What does this show about the Jewish leaders?

How did they inadvertently cause even stronger proof of the resurrection of Christ?

4. Can God's purposes ever be thwarted?
   Answer based on the following scriptures:

   Job 5:12-13:

   Proverbs 19:21:

   Isaiah 46:9-10:

   How has God shown Himself sovereign in your life?

5. Who rolled the stone away?
   (See Matthew 28:2-4)

6. Describe the story the keepers were paid to tell later.
   (See Matthew 28:11-15)

7. Describe what the women saw in the tomb. (v.5)

   What news and instruction did the angel have for them? (v. 6-7)

   Why was Peter singled out?
   (See Luke 22:59-62)

Are you living in condemnation today over a sin you have already been forgiven for?
Accept the tender love and forgiveness that our Savior has for you!

8. Read John 20:1-10.
   What news did Mary Magdalene have for Peter and John?

   What was the scene they came upon? (John 20:5-7)

9. To whom did Jesus first appear? (v.9; John 20:11-18)

   Did they realize what had happened in the light of biblical prophecy?

   Should they have recalled scriptures? Summarize these:

   Job 19:25:

   Psalm 16:10:

   Psalm 68:18:

   What would they say later?

   Acts 2:24:

   2 Peter 1:16-19:

   1 John 1:1-2:

10. Why do you think Jesus appeared first to Mary Magdalene?
    Give scriptures!
    Example: Luke 7:46-47

11. What was the reaction of the disciples to Mary's news? (v.12)

    How was this typical of them?
    Refer to the following:

    Matthew 16:5-9:

    Mark 4:40:

    Mark 9:19:

12. What assurance do we have for the times when our faith fails?

    Luke 22:32:

    Hebrews 7:25b:

13. Read verse 12-13, and Luke 24:13-35.
    How was Jesus known to them?

    Write some of your favorite Old Testament scriptures that speak of Jesus.

14. Describe Jesus' next appearance, as described in v.14, and John 20:19-29.

    Which disciple was particularly disbelieving?

    How are we as believers particularly blessed today?
    Answer from the following:

John 20:29:

2 Corinthians 5:7:

1 Peter 1:8:

15. Coming to a conclusion in our study of Mark (and the other gospels) consider and count the cost:

    What is your assignment from the Lord Jesus Christ?
    (Refer to v. 15; Matthew 28:19-20)

    Are you carrying out your assignment? How?

16. Where is Christ now? (v.19; Acts 1:9-11)

    Summarize:
    Hebrews 1:3:

    Hebrews 7:25-26:

    Hebrews 8:1:

We thank You, dear Lord, for your Word which gives us so much assurance of who You are, and who we are in You!

We pray that we might have the mind of the Son of Man, who came not to be ministered unto, but to minister, and to give His life a ransom for many.

www.ingramcontent.com/pod-product-compliance
Lightning Source LLC
LaVergne TN
LVHW072125060526
838201LV00071B/4978